THE FUTURE OF FUNDRAISING

ADAPTING TO CHANGING PHILANTHROPIC REALITIES

JAMES M. LANGLEY

ACADEMIC IMPRESSIONS | 2020
DENVER, CO

James M. Langley

Published by Academic Impressions.

CR Mrig Company. 5299 DTC Blvd., Ste. 1400. Greenwood Village, CO 80111.

Copyright © 2020 James M. Langley.

Cover design by Brady Stanton.

All rights reserved.

No part of this book may be reproduced, or stored in a retrieval system, or transmitted in any form or by any means, electronic, mechanical, photocopying, recording, or otherwise, without express written permission of the publisher.

For reproduction, distribution, or copy permissions, or to order additional copies, please contact the Academic Impressions office at 720.488.6800 or visit:

www.academicimpressions.com

Academic Impressions

ISBN 978-1-948658-17-1

Printed in the United States of America.

THE FUTURE OF FUNDRAISING

MORE FROM JAMES LANGLEY

Get James M. Langley's bestselling guides *Fundraising for Presidents, Fundraising for Deans, Fundraising for Boards,* and *Comprehensive Fundraising Campaigns: A Guide for Presidents and Boards,* at:

https://www.academicimpressions.com/product/jim-langleys-fundraising-guides-university-leaders/

JAMES M. LANGLEY

CONTENTS

INTRODUCTION	1
CHAPTER 1: UNDERSTANDING AND ADAPTING TO NEW PHILANTHROPIC REALITIES	8
Underlying Reasons	14
The Present Tense	17
Adapting without Overreacting	21
CHAPTER 2: TOWARD MORE SUSTAINABLE FUNDRAISING PRACTICE: IF YOU'RE IN A HOLE, STOP DIGGING	24
Belief in Infinite Resources	27
Oversimplifications	27
Ego	28
Perception Lagging Reality	36
CHAPTER 3: A BETTER MODEL OF FUNDRAISING	42
The Traditional Institutional Model	46
The Purpose-Driven Model	50

Overcoming Barriers to Change	59
Conclusion	66

CHAPTER 4: ORGANIZING FOR NEW REALITIES — 68

Mission Advancement	77
Constituent Relations	78
Constituent Research and Communication	79
Volunteer Recruitment and Management	82
Donor Retention	82
Donor Acquisition	87

CHAPTER 5: THE ESSENTIALITY OF COLLABORATION — 96

Case Study	96
Lessons Learned	122

CHAPTER 6: RETAINING DONORS THROUGH IMPROVED ACQUISITION AND RESPONSIVENESS — 134

CHAPTER 7: NURTURING AND DEEPENING DONOR RELATIONS — 154

CHAPTER 8: ACQUIRING NEW DONORS — 180

Acquiring Alumni Donors — 194

Acquiring Individual Donors — 200

Acquiring Parents — 209

Acquiring Foundation Support — 211

Acquiring Corporate Support — 213

Common Denominators of Effective Donor Acquisition — 222

CHAPTER 9: BUILDING A MORE ATTUNED AND RESPONSIVE CULTURE — 229

High Impact Initiatives — 234

Alignment of Interests — 235

Partnership Formation — 236

CHAPTER 10: ACQUIRING CONSTITUENTS — 249

CHAPTER 11: EMOTIONAL INTELLIGENCE — 266

Prospect Engagement — 271

Events — 272

Stewardship — 274

Controversies/Crisis Management	278
Volunteer Recruitment and Management	279
Research	281
Prospect Profiles	282
Conclusion	287
APPENDIX: BUT WHAT ABOUT ALL THOSE OTHER "SECRETS OF SUCCESS"?	**290**
Technology and Data	290
The Importance of Building Relationships with Donors	292
Storytelling	293
Donor Centrism	294
Splashy Presentations	295
Splashy Events: The Flaws with Fundraising Events	296
Conclusion	297
Additional Reads	299
ABOUT THE AUTHOR	**301**

THE FUTURE OF FUNDRAISING

JAMES M. LANGLEY

INTRODUCTION

This book was begun before the outbreak of COVID-19 and finished at the peak of it. If it is read when few remember the virus, there will still be a lasting lesson that can be taken from it. It is that when the public sees people performing heroic, selfless deeds—as those performed so inspiringly by many frontline healthcare professionals—their trust in institutions is restored, their appreciation and gratitude soars, and their philanthropy rushes forward.

The fruit of philanthropy grows from the seeds of good deeds. Without philanthropy, fundraising would not be possible. Without people willing, wanting, or feeling morally obligated to give, fundraising appeals would fall on deaf ears. We've never imagined the possibility of the absence of philanthropy because we have been the easy beneficiaries of it for so long. The seeds of it can be found in centuries past, but it flourished in the New World in places where people were highly interdependent. They helped one another build barns and houses of worship, raise crops and husband livestock, sew quilts and preserve food, and provided solace in difficult times. While the same range of human behaviors we see today existed then, the demands of survival loomed larger and closer, so the dangers of selfishness and the advantages of collaboration were more apparent.

When they survived hardship, their faith deepened and their gratitude swelled. When they began to thrive, some concluded they had enough for themselves and began to ask how they might help others, as their faith had called them to do. Some, seeing a new world of possibility, began asking how they could help build a more enlightened, more just, and more prosperous society. At least, that's how they were at their best. At their worst, they failed to apply the same principle to the indigenous, the enslaved, those they deemed to have fallen, and those that challenged or were not well-served by their norms. And yes, some, including some of the most prosperous, deeming their success largely or solely attributable to themselves, became less faithful, less grateful, and less inclined to give of themselves to help others or build a better society. It was ever thus and will ever be.

The grateful, however, so outnumbered the "self-made" that they formed a culture of philanthropy where the example of it was so great, so omnipresent, that giving became a norm, one that influenced the thinking and behaviors of the majority. That culture and ethic of philanthropy proved powerful, influencing those of faith, nominal faith, and no faith. The unifying principle of philanthropy often minimized or muted religious, regional, ethnic, and other cultural differences. At our best, we worked across ideology, idiosyncrasy, ethnicity, and social strata in pursuit of practical solutions and shared ideals. We sought to cement and sustain our values by building and contributing to institutions. Indeed, we came increasingly to think of philanthropy less in interpersonal or intra-community terms and more as the means of supporting institutions. Those institutions—including schools, colleges, and universities—seeing the faith placed in them and witnessing waves of gratitude arising from the good deeds they did, spoke to their adherents as a pastor to a devoted congregation: "Give so that we might sustain operations." "Give so that we might build a more beautiful structure." "Give so that we might be even better at what we do." Implicit in those appeals was a tacit assumption: "You understand and appreciate the good we do. You trust us to make the right decisions. Here's what we need."

Ah, but somewhere along the way we began to lose faith in institutions. Public confidence in all institutions, as seen in indices such as the Edelman Trust Index, has been eroding for decades. The reasons for it are many and yet to be learned. The most obvious seems to be the tendency of institutional leaders to become removed from the lived realities of their constituents, particularly as they grow in size and stature. They begin making more and more decisions, believing they are acting on their constituents' behalf and with the assumption that those decisions will all meet their adherents' unquestioning approval. The more they assume, the less they listen. Gaps begin to open – gaps between what they hope from their supporters and what their supporters hope from them. On the societal side, the widening of the trust gap may have been fueled, in part, by rising tides of individualism and the increasing inhabitation of virtual worlds that satisfy sensory appetites but, in and of themselves, build only ephemeral human bonds, evanescent experiences, transitory commitments, and less engagement in activities that cause us to subordinate individuality to achieve a greater common good.

Yet, as some great philosopher once said, "It is what it is." Institutional leaders that blame societal trends for their struggles or demise forget that no institution can hope to long survive, much less thrive, if it does not adapt and re-establish its relevance in the eyes of each generation. No institution can hope to be effective at fundraising, therefore, without picking up on and adapting to changing philanthropic behaviors – which are invariably shaped by changing attitudes, and none more significant in this instance, than the erosion of trust. The second is the segmentation of societal interests and tastes, which can be seen in every area of human consumption. One need only go to their favorite coffee shop, hover around the spot where people place their orders for ten minutes, and listen to the wide variety of orders placed. Virtually no one orders just "coffee." Yes, nearly everyone orders coffee, but the coffee shop has learned it will be far more profitable if it customizes the core product to satisfy a wide variety of individual interests. Café Alma Mater, for a long time, offered one option to its alumni – "You give; we decide how it will be used." That menu expanded open the years to include preferred giving options such as, optimally, unrestricted endowment, then scholarships, faculty support, and capital improvements.

Yet the philanthropic tastes of alumni, and those of the larger giving world, were expanding more rapidly than the options provided. And more and more were waving off the entire menu of giving options and saying, "Here are my preferences. How can you accommodate them?" And fewer and fewer alumni, saddled with more and more debt, felt less and less inclined to frequent the café. For some, the whole experience left such a bad taste in their mouths that they began staying away in droves. Many of those cafes are still open. Too many are measuring their success by fewer and fewer patrons making larger purchases, remaining oblivious to increasing number of patrons they lost and the ones they never attracted. They insist that their pricing strategies, choices, and marketing are working based on sales receipts but do not acknowledge that the vast majority of their patrons are getting older and that fewer middle-aged and young patrons are showing up. They do not acknowledge that a consistent loss of volume will, at some point, drag down the bottom line – and keep it down for a long time. We can no longer be content with taking credit for what works some of the time, but less of the time, while failing to acknowledge the greater loss and damage being done by failing to adapt to new attitudes, new behaviors, and new philanthropic realities. Therefore:

- We must respect and respond to shifting sensibilities of our donors lest we contribute to a greater contraction of philanthropic participation in our society;

- We have an obligation to expend the resources available for fundraising in the most efficient and productive ways possible; money wasted on misguided efforts is money taken away from mission realization; and

- We must create conditions that allow those who work for us to use their time and talents most rewardingly and productively. If we send good people on ill-designed, unrealistic fundraising forays, their faith in and willingness to commit themselves to our causes slips, and with it, our ability to retain the most capable and conscientious among them.

Yes, even with the mounting evidence of the consequences of ineffective fundraising or fundraising that clamors for more, yet has little mission advancement to show for it, we still see many organizations jumping to false assumptions and clinging to dated practices. Why is this so and how can all of us – board members, presidents, advancement staff and others – become agents of positive change? We must first become agents of philanthropy itself by recognizing it is not infinite and inexhaustible. We must acknowledge the need to nourish it over time – not just extract as much as we can, as soon as we can, while offering as little in return as we can get away with.

In particular, institutional leaders must learn to question, challenge, and ultimately eschew tactical, transactional, and even gimmicky approaches that generate support from donors some of the time but do not sustain donors' interest over time nor come close to optimizing their greater philanthropic potential. To make matters worse, some of those same practices cause other donors to cease giving to institutions employing such practices, because they deem them uninteresting, beneath the dignity of an educational institution, or otherwise off-putting, if not alienating. This book, therefore, must not only acknowledge and share what we have learned from the most earnest and ethical practitioners, it must point out where we have gone wrong, where we have allowed myths to proliferate without countering with research and fact, we have let our egos get in the way of our better judgment and where we should have spoken up sooner about depletive, destructive practices.

The purpose of this book is to document changing philanthropic behaviors and expectations and then describe the strategies and tactics that will allow fundraising operations and institutions to detect and catch the prevailing winds in their sails and thereby expedite the advancement of their missions and sustain, if not gain, donor trust. Throughout, we will contrast old, increasingly ineffective ways with current and emerging best practices, as well as how we must organize ourselves and how we must create new models of collaboration to develop a more adaptive craft, one that will lead us more certainly to more sustainable shores.

In Chapter 1, we will explore:

- How and why philanthropic behaviors have changed
- Why some donors have simply ceased to give to institutions
- Why encroaching realities have been ignored or misread
- Why it is important to adapt but not overreact to new philanthropic realities

CHAPTER 1
UNDERSTANDING AND ADAPTING TO NEW PHILANTHROPIC REALITIES

Philanthropic behaviors—who gives, how they give, when they give, why they give and what they give to, and where they give the most—have changed dramatically over the past 30 years. Consider:

According to the Lilly Family School of Philanthropy at IUPUI, the U.S. has experienced "continued attrition in the percent of American households who gave to charity, from about two-thirds in 2000 to just over half in 2016…. The 20 million fewer households that gave to charity represents a decline of about 13%." All indicators are that this trend has continued after the data collection for this study concluded in 2017—and will continue in the years ahead if there is not a more significant shift toward sustainable practices.

The historical significance of, and the ongoing impact from, this decline is enormous for many reasons including:

- The U.S., in terms of the percentage of households giving to institutions and in amounts of money given annually, is the most philanthropic culture in the world.

THE FUTURE OF FUNDRAISING

- The steady decline in giving households is unprecedented when compared to the previous century or the time in which we have been able to measure that behavior.

- The data underscores the likely persistence—if not acceleration—of these trends given that the highest rates of participation by the oldest generations are not being emulated by younger generations.

Higher education has been among the most adversely affected segments, a reality presaged by a 30-year decline in alumni participation (the percentage of all alumni giving back to their alma mater annually). That impact, relative to all giving by sources, can be seen below.

	USA	**HIGHER ED**
Individuals	79%	44% (26%*)
Foundations	16%	31%
Corporations	5%	15%
Other		10%**

Percentage of the total who are alumni.
** Representing organizations, most of which are churches.

This comparison shows that higher education has been more adversely affected by these trends in that it has lost support from the largest source – individuals, which is also the most productive and sustainable source of giving, in that loyal individuals, or those retained by institutions over a decade or more, have been the largest source of major gifts and estate gifts. Moreover, the individuals who have stopped giving are alumni, who were once a college or university's largest and most predictable source of support. This fact is a major clue as to what is precipitating such significant change – the lessening loyalty, gratitude, or "giving back" as primary giving motivators. Some surmise that more and more alumni have chosen to give through family foundations, which means the loss of alumni support may not be as severe as it appears. Yes, the "foundations" category does include family foundations, but the number of alumni giving through family foundations is small. Yes, some alumni are giving through them as opposed to giving directly to their alma maters, but they constitute only a small percentage of the total and do not account for the far larger loss of sustained alumni giving.

These realities have been long in the making while their persistence and the encroaching, accumulating consequences have been largely ignored by many educational leaders, in most of the trade publications, and on the agendas of most major conferences. In particular, there has been too little acknowledgement of or willingness to grapple with increasingly troubling indicators, including:

- Declining alumni participation over three decades to the point where less than one in ten alumni give back to their alma mater (a reality often shrugged off as "a national trend").

- Ballyhooing "record years" and increases in the total amount given to higher education in recent years (dollars up) without acknowledging the increasing donor attrition (donors down).

- Ignoring the unevenness of fundraising gains and the fact that much of that was attributable to fewer elite institutions attracting larger gifts from fewer, older, wealthier donors (a recent CASE report on higher education campaigns reveals that 78% of the total giving is now coming from 1% of the donors).

Further, even the giving behaviors of those individuals who continue to give to higher education has changed significantly. According to Reheer, a donor analytics firm, the kinds of committed donors "who made campaign growth possible in the 1990s are aging out of prospect pools. And, the donors stepping up to replace them are a smaller and considerably older group. The last 30 years of donor performance reveals some alarming trends." The Reheer analysis then offers the following evidence:

- *Less frequent donations.* The average number of years of giving before becoming a (committed) donor in 1980 was 7; now, it's 20. Moreover, the median age for a (committed) donor in 1980 was 44.5; now, it's 62. Put simply, potential big donors are waiting longer to give and they're getting older before they do.

- *A shrinking donor segment.* There has been a 30% decline in the number of middle-aged donors over the past 20 years. Much of the focus has been on younger alumni and would-be mega donors, while donors 30-50 years old have been largely ignored.

- Big donors are waiting longer. The median age of first-time "Top 100" donors increased from 53 to 67 between 1980 and 2017. So, your mega donors are waiting 14 years longer to achieve giving levels schools have grown accustomed to. This reality could significantly impact any current and future campaigns.

Finally, even the ways in which, and the purposes to which, donors choose to give has and continues to change. Traditionally, higher education has expended most of its persuasive energy on making a case for unrestricted support or "at the president's discretion," both in terms of annual giving and for the sake of endowment building. In the latter instance, institutions have stressed the importance of endowments as a way of preserving excellence during economic downturns and to afford future leaders optimal discretion in responding to unfolding opportunities. Absent that, fundraising appeals urged donors to help them strengthen certain pillars of institutional distinction—usually in this order—capital improvements, student support, faculty support and programmatic support. Dollar goals were assigned to each category, but few specifics offered—other than, for instance, the number of endowed chairs to be funded under the faculty support heading. Despite the fervent arguments still being made by many institutions for support of these purposes, donors are showing less and less interest in them.

For instance, giving to unrestricted endowments has declined dramatically while giving for capital improvements has declined steadily to the point where fundraising for major structures is increasingly dependent on very large gifts from very few donors. Student support, on the other hand – particularly when placed in the context of student success, individual or collective – holds its appeal within a declining market segment of donors. Finally, requests for programmatic support, when couched as ways that institutional strengths can be leveraged to achieve some larger societal gain, are attracting some of the most significant gifts, including some of the largest in the history of higher education.

In addition, the vast majority of donors are not giving to categories advertised in various fundraising appeals. They are giving for much more specific purposes and specific initiatives with targeted outcomes. For example, one donor might be motivated to create a lecture series in the name of a favorite professor, while another may create a fund for experiential learning in environmental studies based on his belief that a greater commitment will be made to the environment if more students have more hands-on opportunities to grapple with real issues, while still others may endow chairs in the Mandarin language because they believe mastery of it will be essential to business success or world peace. All those gifts may be subsumed under the heading of "faculty support" and so reported in institutional communications, but none of those donors gave because the category was created, advertised, or advocated for; they gave out of personal interests, experiences and convictions. Uninitiated trustees, deans, faculty members, and others may read institutional reports and assume that the reason donors gave the aforementioned gifts was because the campaign literature made such a persuasive case for "faculty support" and, therefore, argue for more of the same, without realizing that the case may have had little if anything to do with any of those gifts. Indeed, most donors who give to most campaigns, do not do so because an institution is in a campaign, and do not give in certain ways because the institution has asked them to, but in ways that their lives and careers have taught them to be important.

Underlying Reasons

If we explore the underlying reasons behind these trends, we can not only see why those trends are likely to persist but also why adaptation to new realities will become essential. One of the largest societal forces at work is a global phenomenon – declining public trust in all institutions. Donors once loyal to their alma mater have begun acting more and more on their personal convictions, demonstrating a stronger and stronger tendency to favor organizations that shared their convictions and offered specific plans for acting on them. Some, quite tragically, as noted earlier, simply stopped giving to institutions altogether.

As trust in institutions declined so did emotional connections and the number of people who drew a significant portion of their identities from the institutions with which they affiliated (e.g., those who might routinely wear their school's colors or, say they "bleed" their school's colors). Attendance at events and activities offering red meat to rah-rah loyalists, such as homecoming and reunion, declined at many institutions – an early and persistent indicator of new realities.

The Future of Fundraising

Challenges to institutions have come not just in the form of declining trust but in the edgy attitudes of assumption-busting competitors known as entrepreneurs. In this new world, even longstanding blue-chip corporations, including those who had been in the Fortune 500 for decades, have found their stature threatened if not surmounted by more market-sensitive, risk-taking entrepreneurial firms. Some of those start-ups leapt into the Fortune 500, 100, and 10 within a decade or two, proving that even powerful brand identity and deep pockets are no match for ideas and innovations that resonate with changing tastes and behaviors.

Just as corporations in the 1980s and beyond found themselves challenged and outflanked by entrepreneurs, who saw opportunity where they did not and who moved at a speed they could not, often taking risks they dared not, so too did educational institutions find themselves and their long-held assumptions challenged by entrepreneurial thinking – both within their own constituencies, including alumni and parents who began cajoling institutional leaders to "think outside the box," and without from competitors keen on proving that there were more cost-effective ways of imparting more relevant skills to larger numbers of people.

Where donors had once been content to give their money without restriction, with the belief that the president would know how to apply it to the institution's "highest and greatest use," growing numbers of more self-directed, less trusting, or more entrepreneurial donors began restricting their gifts to disciplines, programs, or initiatives that resonated most with their personal convictions or professional interests. The more donors gave, the more inclined they were to restrict their gifts to specific purposes – which provided a significant fundraising clue: You can raise much more by discovering what donors want to achieve than by trying to convince them to give to what the institution most wants.

Entrepreneurs and the wealth they accrued are proving to be an increasingly powerful force in philanthropy. Many scoff at requests for endowments, seeing them as a way of buffering institutions from market forces rather than adapting to them. They challenge building plans, including the cost per square foot, the adaptability of those structures to evolving purposes, and whether they are temples of privilege or facilitative of innovation. Conversely, as institutional representatives grasp the philanthropic mindset and speak a language that entrepreneurs understand – including how their strengths can be leveraged to provide a greater societal return or where innovation can anticipate an emerging need – they are able to broker some of their largest gifts ever. Indeed, in many instances entrepreneurs are proving themselves to be more generous – under the right circumstances – than the cherished loyal Boomer.

However, whereas Boomers gave to institutions to support institutional purposes, entrepreneurs and those who consider themselves investment-oriented give through institutions in pursuit of significant, sustained societal impacts. The impact of entrepreneurs can and will be seen more vividly in that incredibly powerful segment of the philanthropic pyramid – that 1% of donors who provide 78% of all support given to American higher education. Loyal Boomers will continue to decline in numbers while Entrepreneurial Donors will play an ever-stronger role in the future. Unfortunately, most organizations remain too reliant on Loyal Boomers and too ill equipped to compete for support from generous but discerning Entrepreneurial Donors.

TRUE BELIEVER	ENTREPRENEURIAL DONOR
Motivated by deep personal gratitude	Motivated by "better world" ideas
Loyal donor (15+ years of giving)	Gives to different orgs but for similar purposes
Significant, substantive volunteer service	Avoids serving on standing bodies
Likes and trusts your CEO	Intrigued by one of your thought leaders
Broad talents and interests	Deep technical abilities
Other family members are also giving and/or involved	Cares about institutional agency not personal connections
Consumes institutional materials	Wants to see a project's business plan
Holds sway in the local community	Holds sway in influential, highly specialized field

The Present Tense

Out of this mix of entrepreneurial challenges to traditional thinking and growing mistrust of institutions in general, there has emerged a deeper set of concerns about the future of higher education itself. These concerns have been amplified by powerful demographic shifts that have left and will leave educational institutions with far fewer students from which to choose and, therefore, fewer dollars with which to operate. Institutions, once accustomed to sorting through ample piles of student applications, have seen those stacks decrease while the demand for financial assistance has increased. The availability of financial aid, therefore, has become more critical to maintaining market shares of the kinds of students many institutions had become to expect – and tout. Schools characterize the difference between what they are charging and what families are willing to pay as the "discount rate." Economists might call that a euphemism for an over-priced, over-supplied, declining market. Many educational leaders have concluded that the best way to cover that gap is to ask for more private support for financial aid. However, many debt-burdened alumni are less than receptive to those calls and complain, "My alma mater does little to reach out to me besides asking for money."

Rather than cut mass to protect quality as these persistent demographic realities encroach on fixed assumptions—admittedly extraordinarily difficult to do, many institutions seek to put a bigger patch on the problem by tasking their fundraising operations to do more. While many donors have and will continue to respond to requests for scholarships and financial aid, some of the most significant and discerning are asking tougher questions including:

> "Will the money you raise for financial aid increase the total amount available to students, or will the school use them as

The Future of Fundraising

> replacement dollars?" (i.e., "Will it 'back out' the support it has provided as new gifts come in?")
>
> "If the school keeps raising tuition, won't the value of my scholarship endowment continue to erode?"
>
> "Even if you raise this amount, can the school compete with financial aid packages being offered by other schools with bigger endowments and deeper pockets?"
>
> "Do we really want students who we have to pay to enroll?"
>
> "Doesn't the rising discount raise real issues about your underlying business plan?"
>
> "Why would I create a large endowment when we're not sure how long the school, in its present form, is going to be here?"

Few institutions are immune from such questions. While most brag about the critical thinking skills they imparted to their students, many are surprised when their alumni verify that claim with the questions they put to their alma maters. Some institutions with forthright leaders answer these questions openly and honestly. Some institutional leaders are less than forthright about issue like "replacement dollars." Some become irritated by them and tell their fundraisers to avoid difficult donors. Some don't even know how frequently these questions are being asked. These kinds of questions, however, aren't going away. With greater shrinkage in the student market, including an 18% decline in 2026, will come greater challenges to traditional fundraising approaches and stopgap strategies. The more institutions respond to enrollment declines by increasing the amount of their financial aid packages, the more they will task their fundraising operations to produce more financial aid or "scholarship" support. The more fundraising operations seek to cover the gap between what an institution charges and what families can and/or are willing to pay, the more donors will come to realize that they are not creating more opportunities for more students, only patching over the issue of sustainable financial viability. The more institutions assert the importance of financial aid support, the more donors will ask what they are doing to contain or cut costs in an effort to preserve or strengthen their essential value proposition. Institutions that have not made difficult decisions – including cutting weak programs or those that no longer attract sufficient numbers of students, or who have not developed other sources of revenue to offset tuition costs – will find it extremely difficult to secure enough financial aid support to stay afloat.

Financial aid or scholarship support serve as proxy for understanding the unfolding challenges and the decisions that must be made. Donors will continue to support scholarships at institutions where it can be shown that every new scholarship underwrites yet another promising student or provides scholarship endowments that demonstrably increase the quality and/or number of students to be served. They will not continue to provide scholarship support where no real difference is made in the quality or target socioeconomics of the student body, and where the value of endowments is consistently eroded by tuition increases that outpace endowment earnings. And this will be particularly true of that 1% who now provides 78% of the fundraising totals.

Adapting without Overreacting

The emergence of new philanthropic realities has not eliminated older ones, only diminished their frequency, which causes some to be confused about what is really happening. Yes, some donors are still giving without restriction, but their numbers are in steady decline. Yes, some are even creating unrestricted endowments, but they are in the distinct minority and continuing to decline. Yes, some people continue to support capital improvements, but they represent a smaller and smaller portion of those giving to overall educational purposes.

The simple graph below allows us to understand how certain phenomena – be it the number of donors, the number of donors willing to give unrestricted gifts, etc. – can decline slowly but steadily even as new behaviors – such as more discerning donors asking for projections of societal return – continue to increase.

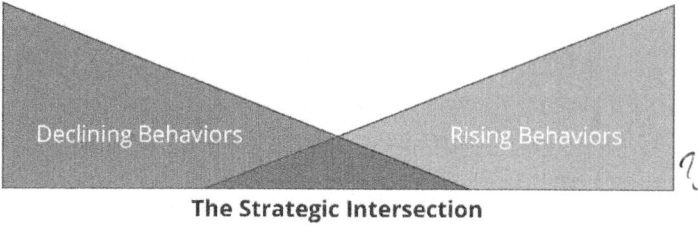

Declining Behaviors | Rising Behaviors

The Strategic Intersection

The trends affecting the future of fundraising are powerful, certain, and inexorable. Yet, many institutional and advancement leaders will fail to acknowledge or adapt to them. They will point to evidence that their traditional approaches continue to work. And, yes, *some* of the old ways will continue to work because loyalists from the Silent and Baby Boomer generations persist in their trusting ways, yet actuarial evidence of their decline mounts with every passing day. Yes, many of those Boomers will be with us for several decades more, but younger generations are exhibiting very different philanthropic behaviors and, notwithstanding wishful thinking, will not start acting like Boomers when they reach a certain age because their lives have taught them very different lessons.

Yes, some of the old ways will continue to work in places where institutions maintained their distinction, integrity, and value and/or where leaders have won the trust of many key constituents. Yet, no institution can remain relevant or optimize its full potential if it does not adapt to emerging realties. It would be unconscionable for institutional leaders to imperil the future of institutions entrusted to their care by clinging to single-dimensional strategies simply because they "seem to be working." They must guide those institutions around eroding pathways, through unfolding passages, and toward more certain footing and, potentially, higher ground.

The key then is to work "The Strategic Intersection" in the next decade, working to both deepen and harvest the goodwill of traditional donors while adopting new capabilities to capture rising philanthropic trends.

THE FUTURE OF FUNDRAISING

In the next chapter, we will discuss:

- How and why fundraising myths came about and how they have led to practices that deplete the philanthropic spirit and cause institutions to lose support and/or sub-optimize their philanthropic potential

- How so many long-standing assumptions about fundraising have not stood up to fuller, more objective examination

- How and why current fundraising perceptions are still lagging new philanthropic realities

- What it will take for institutional cultures to rid themselves of self-limiting assumptions and adjust to new philanthropic expectations

JAMES M. LANGLEY

CHAPTER 2
TOWARD MORE SUSTAINABLE FUNDRAISING PRACTICE: IF YOU'RE IN A HOLE, STOP DIGGING

Adapting fundraising practices to current and emerging realities will require learning new ways and sloughing off old ones, particularly those that have contributed most to donor attrition, donor fatigue, discouragement, or even withdrawal from any philanthropic participation, as has been the case with over 20 million donors in the U.S. since 2000. One of the best places to start that examination is by heeding the advice of Penelope Burk, someone who has monitored and measured trends in the U.S. and Canada over that time and been at the vanguard of the "donor-centric" movement. Her extensive research reveals the most obvious causes:

> Over-soliciting and insisting on unrestricted gifts are largely why 65% of donors who make a first gift never make a second and why 90% or more of donors who start giving are gone within five subsequent appeals. These problems are as frustrating for fundraisers as they are for donors because they are under pressure to ask too often and talk in general, rather than specific, terms about what happens with the money that donors give. Most fundraisers know they could make much more of it if top decision-makers

> had a better grasp on donor motivation and strategic alternatives to bombarding donors with frenetic appeals.

Burk's analysis is particularly cogent in observing the negative trends, the primary causes thereof, and the fact that knowledge often gleaned by frontline fundraisers, doesn't make its way to the top to affect the direction set by "decision-makers." Therefore, nothing will affect the future of fundraising for educational institutions, or that of any nonprofit, more than the willingness of their leaders to become more attuned to and respectful of donor motivation and demotivation.

Anyone who seeks to bring about change in fundraising practice, even when armed with powerful evidence right from donors' mouths, encounters resistant decision-makers whose perceptions are rooted in persistent myths, misperceptions, dated assumptions, and highly unrealistic assumptions about fundraising. Decision makers who cling to those misperceptions, often because they have heard them reinforced so often and for so long, create cultures where false expectations reign which, in turn, lead to a host of ills as the chart on the next page demonstrates.

Because these misperceptions are so deep-seated and persistent, they will not be easy to overcome, but enlightened practitioners can help debunk them and diminish their impact by better understanding where they came from and how they took root. This will allow us to deal with them in a more compassionate and tolerant manner while making sure we do nothing to contribute to their furtherance.

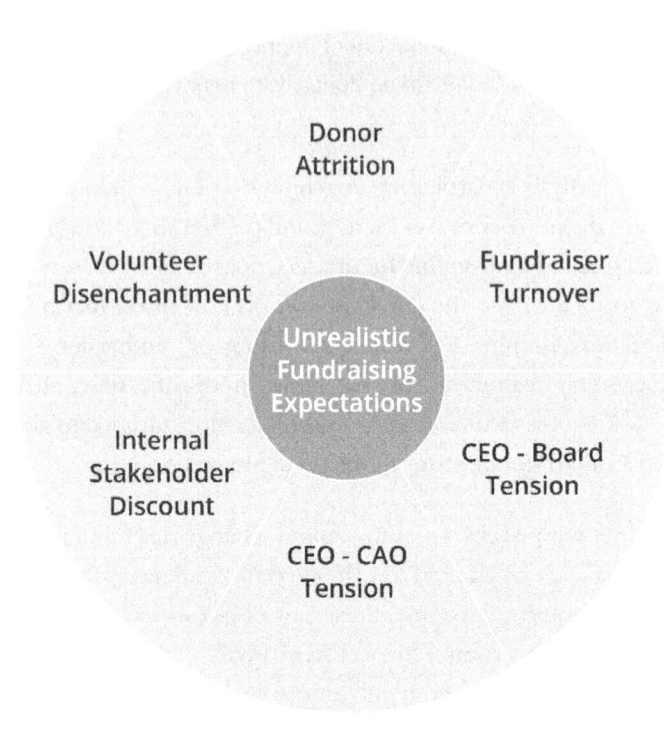

Diagram: Central circle "Unrealistic Fundraising Expectations" surrounded by: Donor Attrition, Fundraiser Turnover, CEO - Board Tension, CEO - CAO Tension, Internal Stakeholder Discount, Volunteer Disenchantment.

The creation and persistence of fundraising myths, misperception, and unrealistic expectations can be traced back to various phenomena.

1. Belief in infinite resources
2. Oversimplifications
3. Ego
4. Perception lagging reality

Let's take a quick look at each to understand how we got into this situation and, therefore, how we can get out.

Belief in Infinite Resources

One way of understanding why and how fewer households are participating in what was once the greatest philanthropic revolution in human history is to draw a parallel to human management of various natural resources, such as water and minerals. We have a tendency to take them for granted, to extract as much as we can as long as we can until it becomes abundantly clear that they are nearing the point of exhaustion. Then some of us begin to pay heed to those who have been warning us of their finiteness and need to engage in more sustainable practices, while others insist nothing has changed. And, a significant portion of those who show a willingness to adapt and engage in sustainable practices do so not just to preserve a natural resource or "save the planet" but because new practices prove to be more productive and profitable.

Oversimplifications

Plentiful opportunities lead to oversimplifications, which behave like weeds – they take root quickly, grow rapidly, and prove hard to kill. One of the most common was "the major reason people give is because they were asked." That's like saying those who agree to marry do so simply "because they were asked." Yes, a proposal may produce an affirmative response, but how many people get married and stay married simply because the other person asked repeatedly, relentlessly, persuasively, aggressively, or cleverly? Does not the marriage proposal, no matter how charming or disarming, pale in comparison to the process that precedes it, the process that allows both parties to explore the potential of shared values and interests and then conclude their future is brighter together than apart? And haven't many couples entered into long, loving relationships even when the proposal fell short of some romantic ideal? Later, this book will lay out approaches and processes that greatly increase the likelihood of donors entering into philanthropic partnerships with worthy institutions.

Ego

Ego, a quality essential to self-preservation, can easily slip into the means by which we give ourselves more credit than we deserve and, by extension, others less credit than they warrant. We see this in fundraising when we give ourselves, as individuals or institutions, more credit for having raised the money than we do to our donors for having given it. This is most likely to happen in personalities and cultures that place more emphasis on "the ask" than in the deliberative decision-making process that proceeds it—a process that, if executed respectfully and gracefully, greatly increases the probability of successful gift agreements and successful donor relations over time. In addition, ask-oriented individuals and institutions pay much too little attention to the philanthropic quest that precedes the process. Let's make sure we understand both what we mean by the fundraising process and the philanthropic quest.

The Future of Fundraising

The fundraising process begins when someone with fundraising intent contacts a prospective donor and begins exploring the potential of exploring their support. With an annual fund call, that contact usually includes a solicitation, whereas the process that produces a major gift may entail 7-9 interactions over a year a more. That begins with an effort to find common ground and to conclude with a morally, mutually binding gift agreement. When done well, the major gift process unfolds in a series of progressive interactions, each one building on the last, thereby making the solicitation all but a foregone conclusion.

While too little attention has been paid to building a mutually satisfying process, even less attention has been paid to donor receptivity and donor resonance. For example, while philanthropic people receive pleas from many well-intentioned causes, they choose to support some and pass on many others. They are receptive to some causes because they tap into personal concerns and convictions, the roots of which can be found in family values and formative experiences or, in many cases, great suffering. For instance, the person most likely to give most generously to the remediation of a disease or social ill is the person who suffered as a result of it or had a loved one do so. Personal experience makes donors receptive to some causes, somewhat receptive to others, and non-receptive to still others. Effective fundraising, therefore, begins not with mass promotion, but in attempting to align specific organizational aspirations with prospective donors with high degrees of receptivity to them.

JAMES M. LANGLEY

The most effective fundraising processes start when prospects express receptivity but reach their greatest potential when an initiative, and the hope that it resonates at a deep personal level in what Yeat's called "the deep heart's core," causing those prospects to assign their highest philanthropic priority to its realization. We see this when an institution, for instance, proposes to seek the genetic origins of a disease that has afflicted a family for generations, when an organization seeks to support student-veterans in a way that veteran alumni feel was missing when they went through school, or when a school proposes to create or expand an academic program in an area that corresponds to what a donor has long advocated or a nascent field that he or she has pioneered in. In instances where donors consistently act on convictions and passions in their giving choices, we can see, understand, and more gracefully come alongside their philanthropic journey. When we see donors resonate deeply with a cause or purpose and give in extraordinarily generous ways according to their means, we know it is a deeply personal quest. When we see, understand, and propose plausible ways of fulfilling that quest, we can be a party to transformative philanthropy.

Prospects are not passive unfertilized buds waiting for some pollen-laden bee of a fundraiser to show and help them blossom into a beautiful philanthropist. Proof that this reality penetrated the consciousness of many decision-makers can be seen in the expectations enumerated in job descriptions for presidents, school heads, deans, and fundraisers. It can be seen in the reports produced by those officials and their advancement offices, which are chockfull of statements like "we raised xx" rather than "they gave xx," and in which fundraising successes, especially the meeting or exceeding annual or campaign dollar goals, are ballyhooed far more than the remarkable willingness of donors to give of themselves. And it can be seen in the lack of any expression as to how the institutions in question intend to prove their worthiness to those who have so loyally and handsomely supported them. Fundraising goals, in such places, are an end unto themselves and the heroes of the narrative are those artful souls who brought home the bacon. All too often, campaigns seem designed to build the credentials of decision-makers and fundraisers, many of whom then use those credentials to shop for greener pastures. All of this has helped deplete the philanthropic spirit and drive down the volume of giving to institutions.

However, without philanthropy, or the willingness of people to take less for themselves so that they might advance causes greater than themselves, fundraising would not be possible. It is more than ironic, then, when fundraisers and fundraising organizations act as if philanthropy is some deeply embedded ore that would not have seen the light of day nor benefited humans had they not extracted it with their magical arts. To use another metaphor, it is a bit like the person opening their blinds taking credit for the sun that shines in. Pompous self-importance — whether it is engrained in institutional culture, manifested in leaders or fundraisers chosen to represent them or the requests made by them, or apparent in the consultants chosen to guide their efforts — has played no small part in depressing and depleting the more selfless philanthropic spirit in our country. And the inflated claims made by many fundraisers and fundraising organizations over many years have played no small part in the creation of myths about fundraising and the unrealistic expectations piled on anyone with fundraising responsibilities today.

Movement toward a more balanced view of fundraising can be seen in those who have emerged as thought leaders in the field. None, it seems, achieved the stature of Jerold Panas, who brought much insight to the field of professional fundraising, including the importance of listening to and according a deep respect for the dignity and inner drive of every donor and working in close, respectful interpersonal interactions with them. But Panas focused much of his efforts on "Asking." In fact, that was the title of his best-selling book. His other best-selling books included *Mega Gifts*, *Born to Ask*, and *Supremely Successful Selling*. Note the word choices and the emphasis on asking, selling, and the later stages of the fundraising process. When we err on that side, we begin to draw false or weak conclusions from flawed assumptions, such as:

- The more persistent the pursuit, the more the donor will be impressed.
- The bolder "the ask" the better.
- The more charismatic the asker, the more donors will give.

As a result, many people came to believe, and still hold to that belief, the best fundraisers are seize-the-moment seducers. Yet, Penelope Burk's research and that of others who focused on underlying behaviors proves the inverse is much more likely to be true.

The Future of Fundraising

The "ask early and often" school of thought fails to acknowledge:

- At least one quarter of the population doesn't give, no matter how much money they have or how often or how persuasively they are asked.

- Those who give do so out of a value set that is formed long before any fundraiser crosses their path; an extensive Langley Innovations analysis of donors' giving behaviors reveals that donors give for four reasons: (1) Appreciation born of what an institution has done for them or a loved one. (2) Affiliation that makes them feel as if they (including their time and talent) matter to that institution. (3) Agency is demonstrated by that institution in its ability to make significant, sustained contributions to community and/or society. (4) Accountability is demonstrated in the way the institution expends its resources, keeps its commitments, and manages adversity.

- Donors who give at the highest levels do so after having given at more modest levels for 15 years on average, usually to the same institution or similar cause.

  Giving patterns matter

- The most successful solicitations or gift agreements unfold over a year of negotiation that entail at least seven interactions in that time.

  Patience & communication

So, it isn't all about "the ask" and therefore about the asker. Not hardly. It's about the way schools engender appreciation, recruit and capture talent, propose ways to contribute more to society, and keep their promises. Then it's about the way institutional representatives listen to and engage prospective donors and the way they negotiate alignments of interest with them. Indeed, various studies have shown that fundraising success is much less likely to be achieved by the bold askers, who (at the worst) act like "posturing peacocks," and much more so by the "curious chameleons" who listen respectfully and adapt their language and approach to the passions and personalities of various donors.

CURIOUS CHAMELEON	POSTURING PEACOCK
Mid-level introvert	Full-blown extrovert
More comfortable listening than speaking	Loves talking, uncomfortable with silence
Adapts to donors' communication styles and sensibilities	See themselves as "educating" donors
Win donors over with their patient, polite persistence	Secure some gifts but sustain few relationships
Listens to gain insight into donors' animating passions	Listen for what they want to hear
See themselves as facilitators and orchestrators	Fancy themselves masters of persuasion
Collaborates with colleagues	Resent others intruding in their realm
Eager to learn more, no matter how accomplished	Bristle at the mention of "training"
Share information to build shared knowledge base	Hoard information to build personal power base

Panas was exceptionally good at what he did but was reflective of a time when there was less research on donor behaviors and less technical capacity to crunch that data on a large scale and from it develop a deeper understanding of why donors give, why they give for particular purposes, and when some give so generously within their means.

The Future of Fundraising

One advancement thought leader who tried, and in many ways succeeded in, helping us understand how successful fundraising culminated from a longer, more deliberate process was David Dunlop, a former major gift officer from Cornell University, who pioneered the concept and practice of "moves management." That system, Dunlop said, "focuses major gift fundraising on changing people's attitudes so they want to give. To do this, we take a series of initiatives or moves to develop each prospect's awareness of, knowledge of, interest in, involvement with, and commitment to the institution and its mission." The great value of Dunlop's innovation was to help fundraising shops move beyond the broad concept "cultivation," which was difficult to define and impossible to measure, and toward a better defined process that sought to work more systematically with donors through a series of more precise, progressive interactions. Though his work was pioneering and proved to be highly influential, subsequent field experience and research has proven that fundraisers don't change peoples' attitudes, and major gifts are not secured by artful fundraisers moving passive prospects from Scrooge-like beings to philanthropic souls. Indeed, as the years passed, Dunlop himself came to understand and acknowledge this. In 2017, he said, "It can easily be misunderstood, so people start 'making moves' and making a game of moves, rather than really recognizing the process that we're a part of is inspiring people to do the things that we believe they would want to do anyway. Really helping them accomplish what is consistent with their values and interests. It's a different perspective than fancy asking or skillful asking." Good for him. It takes a strong person to back out of an ego trap. His amendment to his earlier thinking is an extraordinarily important one, one that should help move more practitioners and more of the fundraising industry away from statements like "we change people's attitudes" or even that we "inspire" them. We must adopt a less ego-driven approach and acknowledgement that we don't make the non-philanthropic philanthropic or cause the philanthropic to do what they would not otherwise have done had we not shown up. We must acknowledge what we do when we are at our best — recognize, nurture, facilitate, and reinforce philanthropic instincts and intentions. Yes, capable, considerate fundraisers can make a significant role in gift closures and sustaining relationships with donors but conscientious fundraisers and the cultures that support them must always err on the side of giving the preponderance of credit to the donor.

Perception Lagging Reality

Many of the misperceptions of fundraising still lingering in the minds of many decision-makers were formed when it was easier to raise money — when institutions had large reservoirs of goodwill built up over generations, when and where faculty and staff had been able to forge deep, interpersonal bonds with their students, and then propel their debt-free graduates into careers so rewarding that they were soon able to "give back" in gratitude for the difference made by their alma mater. In the minds of those graduates, the value of their education was far greater than the cost, which allowed them to resonate with, and be receptive to, calls to close that gap. Many of the campaigns in the 1980s and 1990s were hugely successful because of those underlying factors, as well as the general economic robustness of the country, particularly the vitality of its middle class, the higher level of confidence that most Americans had in most of their major institutions, and the fact that most alumni had not been asked repeatedly and relentlessly or been subjected to seemingly endless campaigns both in duration and number.

Yet, those attitudes and the conditions that gave rise to them began to change as the cost of higher education soared, the economy sputtered, the middle class stagnated and shrank, and greater wealth concentrated in fewer hands. As enrollments increased to accommodate the echo of the baby boom and the growing belief that a college degree was the key to a better life, fewer students were afforded as much personal attention by their professors, a growing portion of whom were more focused on research than teaching. As tuition increases outran the pace of other goods, services or commodities, more students acquired debt and more alumni struggled to find the economic opportunities enjoyed by their parents, and, therefore, the ability to retire their college debts. Those graduates, finding themselves entreated by their alma maters to "give back" pushed back by saying, "I've given enough already in tuition," according to a path-breaking study conducted by Cindy Cox Roman, president of WIT Consulting. In that same study, conducted in 2011, many alumni revealed that they had "no deep emotional connection" to their alma maters in part because "they do little to reach out to me besides asking for money." It's harder to raise money today because of those and other factors, and it will be even more difficult in the future without a greater acknowledgement of what has gone wrong and a greater determination to rebuilt trust and affinity.

Many decision-makers remain unmindful of factors and forces that have and will continue to weaken their fundraising hand, unaware of the insight we have gleaned as to why and under what conditions donors give most loyally and most generously, and unsophisticated about the tools they have at their disposal to ensure their advancement efforts are effective, efficient, adaptive, and sustainable. Their perceptions will continue to lag current and emerging realities, if not increase the lag, if:

- More board chairs don't educate themselves on philanthropic behavioral patterns or request the same of their fellow board members. Board members remaining oblivious to changing philanthropic realities or feigning or over-estimating their understanding of fundraising foster climates of unrealistic expectations, a major cause of institutional dysfunction, inefficiency, wasteful tension, and staff turnover. Invariably, the worst advice or myth purveying comes from those of means, often of considerable means, who give the least, if at all. The best will come from those who give the most and most loyally, despite their means. Those who practice what they preach will always be better guides than those who speak of philanthropy as something that someone "with more money than me" does. That's why building a culture of philanthropy begins with assembling and retaining a giving board.

- Decision makers don't seek objective, even tough-minded assessments of the barriers and gateways to retaining private support. If institutions don't develop a better understanding of why they are losing donors at any level of giving, they will undercut their aspirations to secure higher levels of private giving. They must no longer accept the pattern of "dollars up, donors down" that has predominated for too long. They must understand that the retained, satisfied (if not delighted) donor is the most likely source, by far and away, of major gifts and estate gifts. They must, therefore, stop asking, "How much money did we raise last year?" and start asking, "How many donors did we retain, and what did we do to ascertain their level of satisfaction?" They must understand that they can only lose so many donors for so long before they permanently imperil the fundraising potential of the institutions they have been entrusted to guide.

- Hiring authorities seek out advancement professionals with a depth of knowledge about the state of philanthropy, as opposed to a glancing knowledge of basic fundraising technique, and behavioral science, rather than gauzy theories based on lore and supposition.

- Senior advancement officials present themselves as constant learners rather than as all-knowing and affronted by any suggestion that they or their operations could become even better.

- Advancement practitioners don't stop boasting of their extractive abilities rather than presenting themselves as orchestrators, facilitators, and aligners – and show how those attributes produce higher levels of sustained support.

- Conference planners don't create more "search for the truth" environments and recruit more "honest strugglers" as presenters rather than supposed miracle workers with silver bullet solutions.

We all need to become more data-driven, but we need to be much more clear about the data we most need. How do we explain the juxtaposition of these two facts:

1. Data is giving us greater insight into philanthropic behavior than ever before.
2. Donor attrition, at a national level and at the level experienced by the vast majority of nonprofits, continues to climb.

Could it be that too many institutions are using the data to pursue the most obvious short-term support but not to analyze and respond to the causes of growing donor disconnection? Could it be too few organizations understand the importance of hiring emotionally intelligent leaders who will seek data that will allow their organizations to build stronger bonds with their donors through more considerate listening and conscientious responding or who will use available data to gain greater insight into the animating passion of each donor they encounter? Data, in and of itself, doesn't, can't, and won't improve fundraising efficiency. Data, when framed by and filtered through emotional intelligence, can, does, and will.

In the next chapter we will show how we can use the wealth of information available us today to:

- Expose the presumptions and flaws in traditional fundraising models.
- Explain how to create a new one that allows us to attract and retain an increasingly discerning and diverse set of philanthropic interests.
- Enumerate the key components of the model and the attitudes and outlooks that will ensure its success.

JAMES M. LANGLEY

CHAPTER 3
A BETTER MODEL OF FUNDRAISING

Models found in many a traditional fundraising texts and training modules have had a tendency to over-simplify how money is raised and to portray the process as fundraiser-driven. Perhaps the most simplistic characterization is this:

Qualify → Cultivate → Solicit

Under this model, a donor might be "qualified" as a legitimate, worthy prospect by a fundraiser who deemed them so after an initial visit. This judgment was made often on the fundraiser's instinct rather than by applying "scientific" criteria gleaned from studies of donors' behaviors. The even greater flaw in the model is the use of the term "cultivate." What does it mean exactly? How can you tell when a prospect had been cultivated enough to solicit? Again, such decisions are often left to the instinct of individual fundraisers. This unfortunately leads to the creation of the deep, dark woods of cultivation into which many a prospect is led and from which too few donors ever emerge. Under this model, supervisors might ask a fundraiser, "Where are we with that prospect?" only to hear "Still under cultivation."

The Future of Fundraising

The cause of seemingly endless cultivation is the result often of fundraisers, chosen on the basis of their likeability, befriending prospects with the assumption that the more prospects grow to like them, the more inclined they will be to give. However, too many fundraisers, understanding how much the relationship with that donor is based on interpersonal regard, are reluctant to call the question lest that friendship be curtailed. Others, assuming they have ingratiated themselves sufficiently, spring the question, often for an amount they think the donor capable of giving usually for some broad institutional purpose. While the latter approach leads to some success, it was largely because the donors have strong, preexisting regard for, and extended relationships with, the institution in question. This approach sub-optimizes the giving potential of many prospects by surprising them with the solicitation and giving them too little time to further educate and engage themselves in the matter.

A less simplistic way of depicting the fundraising process is often represented by this diagram:

Identify → Inform → Involve → Invest

This model is superior to the previous one in that it suggests the need to more carefully identify your best prospects and to establish some consistent predictive criteria for doing so, but the wisdom of "informing" and "involving" prospects before asking them to invest which theoretically serves to heighten their enthusiasm and, therefore, their willingness to give more generously within their means. When done well, particularly in cultures that understand this process could take more than a year, this model produces better results and more satisfied donors. When done less well, "involve" is interpreted as social engagement in institutional activities (e.g., campus or regional events), rather than by informing and involving donors in the program or initiative they would be ultimately asked to fund. When that happens, many donors might feel closer to the institution but still surprised by the solicitation request, which may or may not correspond with their deepest values. As a result, they will be less likely to give as much as they might when a stronger alignment is achieved.

Yet, the model is still flawed in its assumptions of donor receptivity to being informed and involved and in their presumed passivity toward being moved from phase to phase. In was in this context that David Dunlop (and those who came to similar conclusions) made his greatest contributions by showing how a series of progressive "moves" could be customized to each prospect. This approach added more sophistication to the process because it comported with the phases of human decision making. It begins with the dawning awareness of the importance of the issue and then (through dialogue, information sharing, and experiential engagement) one becomes more comfortable with making a significant commitment. Yet, those refinements were too often made in the context of assigning too much to the ability of the fundraiser to engineer and drive the process to get what the institution wanted and too little to the importance of understanding, respecting, and demonstrating how the proposed initiative aligned with prospects' value systems.

The following chart contrasts the traditional institutional model of fundraising with an emerging model that is both more sophisticated and more adaptive to current and emerging philanthropic trends.

The Traditional Institutional Fundraising Model

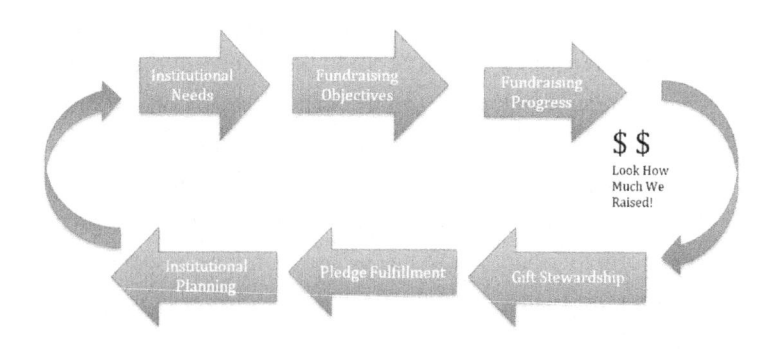

Institutional Needs → Fundraising Objectives → Fundraising Progress

$ $
Look How Much We Raised!

Institutional Planning ← Pledge Fulfillment ← Gift Stewardship

The Purpose-Driven Model of the Future

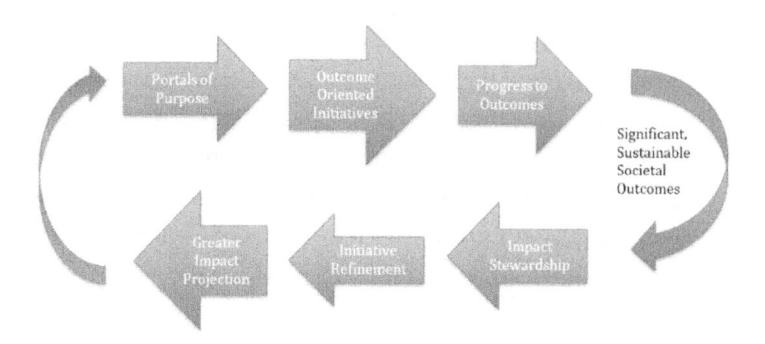

Portals of Purpose → Outcome Oriented Initiatives → Progress to Outcomes

Significant, Sustainable Societal Outcomes

Greater Impact Projection ← Initiative Refinement ← Impact Stewardship

Let us take a closer look at each phase of these models to ensure that we have the depth of knowledge to manage the transition from one to the other.

The Traditional Institutional Model

Institutional Needs

Most fundraising goals, both annual and for campaigns, have been based essentially on internal deliberations as to how private funds, when secured, could be applied to the building of a grander institution. Some institutional needs were the outcomes of strategic planning exercises, many of which were just basic planning exercises that produced a compilation of wants and needs, which were then handed off to the advancement operation to be converted into a compelling case for support.

Fundraising Objectives

The results of these deliberations conducted in splendid isolation formed the basis of a case for support, which spared few superlatives in the belief that adjectival excess was the key to wowing donors into philanthropic submission. The case, sometimes in the form of expensive campaign documents and sometimes in the form of slick fundraising collateral material, was then sprung on unsuspecting prospects. All too often, fundraisers, armed with these materials, were sobered to discover that prospects (who were uninvolved in the discussions about what they should want to give to) proved less willing to give and, eventually, less willing to meet to discuss such scintillating possibilities. The exceptions were the institutional loyalists whose numbers, unfortunately, were waning.

Progress to Outcomes

Thanks to fewer, older, wealthier donors and the enduring loyalty of aging Boomers – and sometimes through creative accounting (extending the life of the campaigns, grandfathering gifts from previous years and previous campaigns, counting all deferred gifts at full face value, etc.) – many institutions were able to report significant progress toward their goals, invariably in the form of dollar amounts, as if there were legions of donors pulling for them to do nothing other than rake in more dough. In some instance, donors were treated to a more fulsome explanation as to which categories (e.g., endowment, capital needs, faculty support, student support, etc.) were being filled out most rapidly. Rarely, if ever, were donors told about the increasing difficulty encountered by many institutions in raising unrestricted endowment and support for capital improvements, especially the most grandiose structures that so missed the fundraising mark that the institution had to eat the resulting debt, often to the tune of millions if not tens of millions of dollars.

Look How Much We Raised

The ballyhooing persisted even as we came to learn that most donors were increasingly asking about the impact of their gifts:

"If you're doing so well and raising so much, why do you need me?" Indeed, younger alumni, seeing big bucks being celebrated at every turn and in every piece of communication, concluded that the more modest amounts they could give would have a greater impact by giving through smaller nonprofits and grassroots causes. To make matters even more interesting, the majority of those giving to institutions were either unmotivated by the fact, or simply unaware, that said institution was in campaign. By seeming to make dollar goals the be-all-and-end-all and by constantly clamoring for more dollars without accounting for the impact of dollars given, many institutions created the lasting perception in the minds of untold alumni that anything said or done in the name of alumni relations (or constituent relations for that matter) was toward one end only – more dollars. This Venus Fly Trap model of engagement sent out subtle and sometime seductive, colorful emanations of wanting to know more about them or to get them involved, but if they took the bait, the fundraising jaws soon closed on them.

Gift Stewardship

Practitioners in this area, under less pressure than fundraisers and less prone to falling into the ego trap of the master mover, often served as the most responsive part of the institution, insuring that donors were thanked in a timely manner, were recognized in fair and consistent ways, and were informed, when applicable, as to the state of their endowments. In fact, these activities defined what we thought of as "stewardship." When more astute advancement practitioners began noting how happy donors became more loyal donors and more generous donors, more efforts were made to thank donors, often profusely and through a variety of media and communication channels. Not as many picked up on the fact that more and more donors were saying they felt sufficiently thanked but relatively uninformed as to the impact of their giving. But moving in this direction – of making sure more donors feel like satisfied investors and enjoy a more substantive role in institutional affairs – is being characterized as "donor relations."

Pledge Fulfillment

Too many organizations assuming, because more dollars had been raised, that everything was hunky-dory in "Donor Land," assumed that the fulfillment of a pledge marked the opportunity to engage donors in the next discussion of institutional needs. Those who picked up on new realities and proved themselves more accountable to their donors found greater donor receptivity; those who did not, did not.

Institutional Strategic Planning

Once one campaign has been completed and/or when new presidents arrive or renew their terms, many institutions go into another cycle of institutional planning, often rolling forward the same set of assumptions as before. In too many instances, their strategic plans are not truly strategic because they do not include an environment scan – including the high likelihood of further demographically-driven enrollment declines, tuition increases outpacing families' ability or willingness to pay, more people questioning if higher education is right for them and looking for other ways to increase their earning power and/or quality of life, and increasing mistrust of institutions and, therefore, institutional thinking. Further, many of these plans will, once again, be developed in splendid isolation and then sprung on unsuspecting prospects, rather than based on needs assessments to determine services that could and should be provided because of growing demand, rather than involve key constituencies in the deliberations including estate donors, loyal donors of ten years or more, accomplished, civic-minded alumni from all walks of life, and other current and potential stakeholders. As a result, they will begin the next round of fundraising with too large of a gap between what they want from donors and what donors want from them – while missing the opportunity to convert marginal stakeholders into more committed ones through open dialogue and substantive engagement.

The Purpose-Driven Model

Portals of Purpose

What current and prospective donors will notice immediately about this approach, in contrast to the traditional one, is first a declaration by institutional leadership to make significant and lasting differences in addressing external needs and opportunities that correspond with their strengths and capabilities. For example, areas in which institutions might seek to make an impact might include:

- Attracting, retaining, and graduating more students from targeted populations, such as those who might represent the rising demographic tide in their catchment area.

- Addressing a host of health issues through the research and public service auspices of their health center, including mitigating the impact of age-related diseases, decreasing rates of infant mortality, health equity, and earlier identification of diseases that are increasing in incidence or severity.

- Improving persistence from pre-k to and through college through the participation of their school of education in a larger coalition of partners.

- Creating or expanding certain majors in response to growing workforce demands.

- Mitigating social ills in their community, including homelessness, poverty, and/or crime.

- Improving food security, product safety, or cyber-security by developing and delivering more sophisticated capabilities to the marketplace.

This approach would not just advertise what donors could do for an institution but what an institution could do for its community, a host of causes, or, in some way, lend its capabilities to improving the human condition. In a world where people continue to lose faith in institutions, this approach would allow schools to show they are not monolithic, remote, or self-serving but adaptive to current and emerging realities. This approach would strengthen the appeal of the institution to current stakeholders who are increasingly specific and self-directed as to where and how they would like to expend their time, talent, and treasure. It would allow institutions to attract post-Boomer generations who have become more cause-oriented and more apt to engage with organizations that operate at grassroot levels to reconsider being engaged with their alma mater or local educational institutions.

Outcome-Oriented Initiatives

If institutions are to impress external constituents with the good they intend to do by recruiting real talent and real selflessness to their cause-oriented portals, they will have to appeal to the growing demand to produce outcomes. This can be achieved by establishing annual and multi-year impact goals for each portal of purpose such as:

- Increase enrollment of first-generation students from local community colleges by 10% in the next two years and their graduation rate by 7%.

- Increase counseling services provided by faculty-led student teams and offered to families with aging, speech-impaired parents by 11% in the next year to help offset the rising demand in targeted communities.

- Expand legal defense services to 75 more homeless people complaining of aggressive policing tactics.

- Research the impact of student athletes returning to their neighborhoods to discourage their younger peers from joining gangs and determine, over a two-year period, which approaches prove most successful.

- Create 12 more deep-dive apprenticeships for students interested in working alongside start-up companies and successful entrepreneurs in the next year.

Developing and projecting such outcomes will require new models of collaboration within learning institutions. For instance, presidents will need to embrace, support, and reward those willing to move out of their comfort zones to develop outcome-oriented initiatives. Advancement leaders will have to work with academic leaders to identify initiatives that showcase institutional strengths that correspond to external interests and, if funded, have a high probability of realizing their stated goals. Advancement leaders will have to provide training for academic leadership, faculty members, and others who are willing to take on these challenges but are inexperienced in making them intelligible and compelling to external parties. Alumni professionals will have to develop new engagement opportunities and venues to allow their constituents to learn more about these offerings and how to lend their talents. Annual giving practitioners will have to scale this approach to allow modest donors to play a significant part in the pursuit of larger goals. Boards will have to move beyond asking how much money was raised in the last quarter or the last year and ask which portals of purpose are most strategic and have the greatest chance of distinguishing the school. They will have asked more about how many new constituents have been engaged and how many more donors have been retained because they have been afforded more satisfying engagement opportunities. In short, virtually every internal constituent will have to adapt to new realities and accept that the greatest gains will come from taking a longer-term view and working more collectively and assiduously toward significant, sustainable societal outcomes.

For fundraising purposes, advancement operations will need to create dialogic venues for kindred spirits and potential funders to come together and discuss what could be – and how they want to be involved. Advancement professionals will need to work with deans, faculty members, and anyone with the potential to emerge as a thought leader or champion of institutionally sanctioned initiatives to develop drafts of white papers which can be used to describe outcome-oriented initiatives in their early stages and to do so in a way that encourages interaction with potential sources of support so that a stronger alignment of interests can be achieved. Discussions around specific initiatives that will allow learning institutions to pursue significant, sustainable societal outcomes should not be limited to major gift donors. They can and should be scaled to alumni relations activities, annual giving engagements, and estate giving. This approach, therefore, should help institutions break down the barriers of specialization within advancement operations, which have tended to sequester donors from one another and treat individual, foundation, and corporate donors in very different ways with the assumption that they have very distinct interests. In fact, all are interested in investing in more tangible outcomes and are increasingly interested in leveraging resources given by others, including state and federal government, for greater societal gain.

Progress to Outcomes

Once outcomes have been projected, and greater alignment of interests between institutional donors and private donors have been forged, including in the form of initial commitments, it becomes essential for institutions to understand the importance of reporting on progress or the lack thereof. In this new world, donors may greatly appreciate being thanked but expect to be informed as to the impact of their giving. Indeed, this whole approach is designed to attract the most substantive volunteers and donors, to respectfully engage them in dialogues as to what is most important to achieve, and to be transparent throughout. Surely, on the face of it, this approach has to be superior and more sustainable than engagements based on promotional froth and vague intentions. Surely, we can see how institutions bent on getting as much as they can as soon as they can, without defining impact, will attract donors with their own angles or donors who will turn into critics when they realize their support has had little or no impact. This, then, is the right step in a more certain way to sustained fundraising success and ensuring institutional regard, reputation, and relevance over time.

Significant, Sustainable, Societal Outcomes

When they are achieved in any form, they become the best form of stewardship and institutional accountability. Donors who see differences being made in areas about which they care the most, and the potential for achieving even more do not complain of "fatigue." That complaint is only heard from those who are asked to give more and more while still wondering what difference they might have made. The attainment of goals enlivens and lends confidence to the whole and begins renewing faith in institutions or, at least, the most productive parts of them. No donor woke up one morning and said, "I just want to give away money." No effective fundraiser woke up one day and said, "I just want to raise money." Both put some greater purpose first, then accepted the responsibility for its higher realization. That's why organizations that best define purpose, and where private support can make the greatest and most lasting impact, do the best job of attracting and retaining both.

Impact Stewardship

In addition to reporting on progress toward goals during periods of pledge fulfillment, it is of immense importance that institutions continue to report on the ongoing impact of initiatives that donors funded years ago. They must think in terms of sustaining "investor confidence." All of this will require ownership of institutional stewardship at the highest levels of the organization.

Initiative Refinement

The vast majority of donors will understand from the outset that outcome-oriented initiatives are experiments. They understand that institutional representatives of those initiatives have pledged to do their all in achieving those outcomes and appreciate their willingness to pursue tangible outcomes. But they will understand that not every goal can be reached. They know their "investments" are not tax deductible if they attempt to treat them as contractually binding, but they will appreciate being brought into each experiment and kept abreast of key developments along the way. They understand that struggles and setbacks will occur but will be keen to learn what initiative directors learned from them and how they will refine their approaches going forward as a result.

Greater Impact Projection

After initial success has been achieved, and/or refinements have been made in initiatives in such a way to foster the possibility for greater impact, institutions have almost a perfect case to present: "Look how much we achieved with what you gave us. With x more, we can extend the impact in these ways." In short, the four most powerful words in a case for reinvestment are "current impact" and "projected impact."

Donors are likely to reinvest if:

- The desired outcomes are specific and plausibly attainable.

- The funds requested to achieve those outcomes are carefully budgeted and without padding.

- The means of evaluating progress, including critical milestones to be reached at certain times, are enumerated.

- Candid updates are promised and met.

- Struggles and setbacks are acknowledged, and necessary course corrections occur.

- Lessons learned in that last experiment are rolled over to the next.

When the doing of good is conducted as an experiment, there are no failures. What is learned from one experiment informs the next and the next. This is the virtuous cycle that every serious philanthropist would love to be a part of.

This approach also conforms to current and emerging philanthropic realities in that donors are increasingly apt to give "starter gifts" or "test gifts" and to advise their peers to do the same. This trend is an outgrowth of donor disappointment with some institutions. So, in the donors' minds, "if some institutions are over-promising and under delivering and some are not, give small gifts initially and see which live up to their promises and which do not and see which prove to be grateful, accountable stewards and which do not." In this new world, those that deliver on their promise position themselves for larger investments. This is also borne out by data in which, even traditionally, we see the largest gifts coming from loyal annual donors of a decade or more and/or highly satisfied major gift donors. However, as the number of loyal donors declines, the satisfied major donor becomes the most likely larger gift donor, the most likely endowment donor, and the most likely estate-giver.

This is not just a new way of fundraising; it is a better way, one that strengthens the negotiating posture of an institution. Institutions that secure the most private support don't ask for anything; they negotiate a value exchange. As a result, they don't have to fawn, whine, wheedle, cajole, humor, acquiesce, or ingratiate themselves with potential investors. They negotiate from a position of relative strength and hold up their portion of the bargain, as the following "old vs. new" comparison suggests.

WEAK POSTURE	STRONG POSTURE
Crying need	Offering greater impact scenarios
Asking for "gifts"	Proposing partnerships
Ingratiating as means of "cultivation"	Brokering organizational strengths
Focusing on "operational support"	Stressing institutional agency
Urging donors to put money in your funds or buckets (e.g. generic endowment)	Offering customized outcome oriented initiatives
Asking for gifts in round numbers (e.g. $10k, $100k, etc.)	Building proposals around carefully crafted budgets
Touting naming opportunities at the outset	Reserving name prominent recognition for proven partners
Conflating gratitude with stewardship	Demonstrating institutional accountability

Overcoming Barriers to Change

As institutions move in this direction, questions, and concerns, they are likely to encounter include the following.

"Doesn't this process open us to higher levels of donor intrusion?"

In fact, it minimizes it because it puts the emphasis on seeking alignment of interests and creating sustainable partnerships of shared purposes, not hustling gifts. Urgency to get as much as we can as soon as we can, and thereby appear "on the make," has opened the door to "on the make" donors or those with heavy personal agendas. This approach requires more research on donors, looking for well-established histories of giving and for other philanthropic propensities to determine if there is the potential to align institutional capabilities with each donor's convictions. This is done before engagement and, therefore, leads to more substantive interactions with more substantive people, those who give the most within their means and manifest the following characteristics:

- Often begin their lives with the least
- Work incredibly hard
- Are very grateful for what life has given them
- Consider themselves lucky
- Believe they have more than enough for themselves
- Draw their greatest lessons from the hardest moments in their lives
- Give so that others will not suffer or struggle as they have

The Future of Fundraising

- Bequeath so much more to the future than they inherited from the past
- Ask little for themselves

The last characteristic causes many organizations to miss them early in their philanthropic journeys as they begin to give, often modestly. Some continue to give modestly all their lives then leave astonishing estate gifts to organizations that they believe have made the most meaningful differences. Those institutions and professionals who look for these qualities and come alongside these donors for the long journey reap the greatest rewards, including the privilege of seeing the very best of human nature.

This approach attracts more substantive donors by calling to more substantive fundraising practices and eschewing superficial ones, as delineated in the following table.

SUPERFICIAL	SUBSTANTIVE
Depict fundraising as a persuasive exercise	Depict fundraising as a listening exercise
Brag about how much they have raised	Express gratitude for having worked with remarkable donors
See fundraising as mass marketing institutional priorities	Share how they aligned donors' interests with institutional aspirations
Rely on the usual fundraising tactics and insist they will work when reinforced by metrics	Advocate more adaptive strategies
Highlight the gifts they have secured	Speak to how they created enduring philanthropic partnerships
Would have you think they work magic	Attribute their success to carefully designed processes and patient persistence
See themselves as prime movers	
Say they remain current by studying best fundraising practices	See themselves as adding value to teams and gaining value from them
	Say they remain current by studying changing philanthropic behaviors

"Does 'donor-centric' mean we're supposed to do everything donors want?"

The donor-centric school of thought, when applied, can be a highly beneficial correction to fundraising practices that have become too institution-centric (all about "our needs") or simply too much about fundraising for fundraising's sake. But we must be careful to not over-correct or misinterpret the proper role of donor centrism. Being grateful, respectful, and accountable to donors, and doing all we can to achieve an alignment of interests with them, is a critical part of the philanthropic equation. However, entertaining and accepting gifts, or gift conditions, that do not strengthen institutional core competencies, or potentially weaken them, is putting the donor delight cart in front of the mission-realization horse. We can't correct one imbalance by creating another one. Creating a lasting and productive philanthropic union requires mutual consideration and the willingness of each partner to subordinate individual interests for the sake of achieving shared goals.

"What about disciplines and departments that represent the fundamentals of lifelong learning? How are they supposed to project greater societal outcomes?"

First, we must understand that most donors are more motivated to give, and will give more, to add value to an institution or enhance its ability to add value to society, rather than to subsidize its day-to-day operational needs. In short, donors are more inclined to give and give more when shown how to enhance the margin of excellence, rather than the margin of survival or simply the continuation of the status quo. Further, in the case of learning institutions, they assume tuition and other sources of income provide the means to become a good school and that you will come to them when you have a plan to take your school, or some part of it, from good to great. The more you ignore or resist these tendencies, and the more you cry need or argue for fairness (donors should give to this department this time because they gave to that department the last time), the more you call your relevance or fiscal viability into question. No one wants to invest in a leaky vessel that's proving increasingly ill-equipped to navigate changing currents or more stormy seas. Even annual donors making modest gifts want to feel as if they are adding value and empowering people to achieve more. Donors at every level of giving are rightly wary of providing funding that would perpetuate institution dysfunction. With that understanding, there is nothing that would prevent the Philosophy or English department from putting forward an initiative that demonstrates how it could bring about a greater societal gain if funded at a certain level. It is simply a matter of making the case for giving through, rather than giving to, that department, as suggested in the following charts.

The Future of Fundraising

GIVING TO:

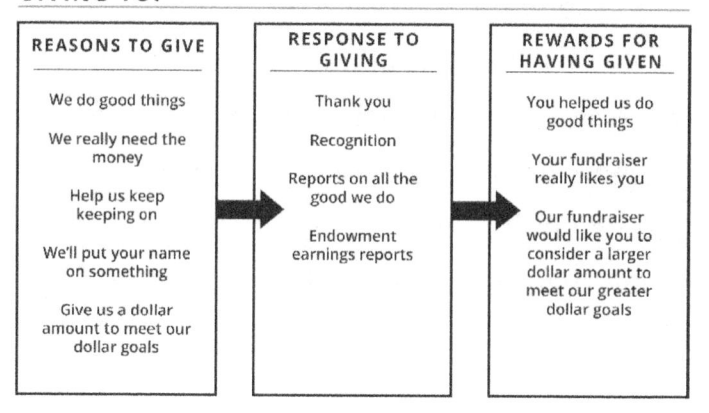

REASONS TO GIVE	RESPONSE TO GIVING	REWARDS FOR HAVING GIVEN
We do good things We really need the money Help us keep keeping on We'll put your name on something Give us a dollar amount to meet our dollar goals	Thank you Recognition Reports on all the good we do Endowment earnings reports	You helped us do good things Your fundraiser really likes you Our fundraiser would like you to consider a larger dollar amount to meet our greater dollar goals

GIVING THROUGH:

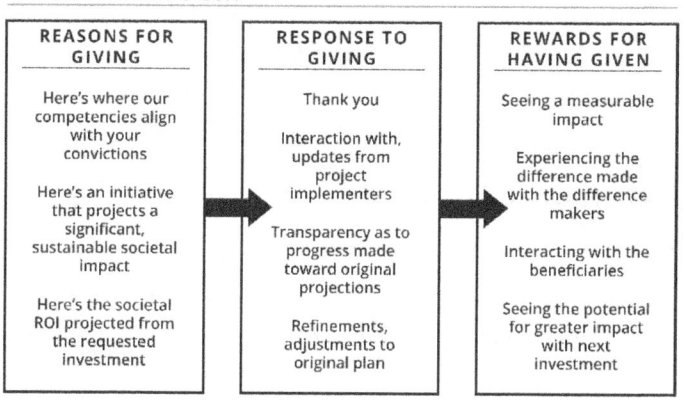

REASONS FOR GIVING	RESPONSE TO GIVING	REWARDS FOR HAVING GIVEN
Here's where our competencies align with your convictions Here's an initiative that projects a significant, sustainable societal impact Here's the societal ROI projected from the requested investment	Thank you Interaction with, updates from project implementers Transparency as to progress made toward original projections Refinements, adjustments to original plan	Seeing a measurable impact Experiencing the difference made with the difference makers Interacting with the beneficiaries Seeing the potential for greater impact with next investment

"The traditional model showcased all institutional needs without attempting to bias the donors' decisions, but the new model presents donors with only the choices deemed most likely resonate with them. Won't that decrease the chances of securing funding for what we need most?"

Donors are increasingly exercising their preferences even when institutions go to great lengths to talk them into funding core needs. This model accepts that reality to ensure that the institution optimizes the giving potential of every prospect. However, core needs can be included in project specific proposals.

Conclusion

Change is never easy. We tend to cling to what we have known because it is familiar and stick to our habits because that is the nature of habits. Yet, if we acknowledge that change is necessary, if we are to stem donor attrition and provide what our most constructive and generous constituents want – greater substantive engagement and more productive philanthropic compacts – we can begin moving more steadily in that direction. The next chapter will:

- Explore the gap between what learning institutions want from their donors and what their donors want from the learning institution.

- Delineate the roles and responsibilities of institutional leaders and advancement professionals in closing those gaps over time.

- Explain how we can organize or reorganize ourselves according to critical functions to ensure we are moving in the right direction.

- Establish the relative weighting of those key functions in ensuring our institutions align with new philanthropic challenges and opportunities.

CHAPTER 4
ORGANIZING FOR NEW REALITIES

WHAT ORGS WANT FOR THEMSELVES	WHAT DONORS WANT FROM ORGS
A culture of philanthropy	A culture of accountability
Major gifts	Major impact
Endowments (to make their future more secure)	Adjustments to constant change
Loyal following	Promise keeping
Impressive facilities	Adaptive structures that facilitate human performance
Reputation	Relevance
To be held in awe	To be heard
Unquestioning trust	Proof of trustworthiness
Event attendance	Substantive engagement
Captive audiences for speeches	Participative problem solving
Giving as a precondition for engagement	Engagement as a precondition for giving

Adapting to new philanthropic realities, both to avoid wasteful, depletive fundraising and to optimize our institutions' ability to produce more significant, sustainable fundraising results requires rethinking how we organize ourselves at every level, including the board, executive team, and advancement operation. In the largest sense, what we must be most attentive to going forward is what we were too inattentive to in the past – the growing gap between what institutions wanted and hoped for from their donors and what donors wanted and hoped for from schools, colleges, and universities. The chart above points to some of those differences.

To stop that widening and begin the process of closing that gap, and thereby moving more steadily to a stronger alignment of interests and purposes, institutional leaders must master one simple but rare skill: better listening. This can be done by *applying classical marketing principles to the practice of fundraising.* Unfortunately, marketing has become synonymous with promotion but marketing defined by the American Marketing Society is rooted in research designed to yield "information used to identify and define marketing opportunities and problems," then develop "the information required to address these issues." Marketing, according to the same source, uses that research to inform an array of "processes for creating, communicating, delivering, and exchanging offerings that have value for customers, clients, partners, and society at large." Even our most storied learning institutions have lost alumni support, a measure of public and constituent confidence, and created more challenges for the future than they inherited from the past. They can correct the course by committing themselves to better listening, including:

- Boards asking for more regular and objective reports on whether constituent confidence is waxing or waning based on any number of indicators including alumni polling, comparing attitudes of students entering the institution to those of students leaving, donor attrition rates, and donor perceptions of stewardship and institutional accountability.

- Boards and presidents insisting on real strategic plans which the aforementioned information is used to inform and shape institutional aspirations and to cause those institutions to take a much more clear-eyed assessment of strengths, weaknesses, threats, and opportunities.

- Boards providing objective analyses to new presidents to ensure they know what they have inherited from their predecessors and what they need to do to leave their successors in a better place.

- Presidents asking for the same reports and interpersonally engaging donors, including the most generous and the most loyal, to listen for perceptions of feeling valued for who they are not just what they give, to where their institution ranks in donors' hierarchy and what they can learn from those they value the most, and ensuring donors that any concerns or frustrations they express will find their way "to the top" and be responded to.

- Provosts or chief academic officers asking deans, department heads, and other relevant academic officials how they are listening to donors who have funded their areas and how they are providing them evidence of ongoing impact.

- Advancement leaders stressing donor retention as their primary goal, thereby requiring designated staff to debrief with first-time donors to discover why they gave and how they hoped the institution would respond; to poll loyal donors on key anniversaries (e.g., 5 years, 10 years, etc.); to ask those in frontline or representational roles to ask questions about their perception of the institution and to record, report, share, and analyze the responses; to ask major donors about their perceptions of the impact of their giving; and to convert traditional one-way vehicles of communications (e.g., phonathons, promotional materials, rah-rah events and speeches) into listening opportunities.

- Advancement leaders hiring staff on their listening abilities, demonstrating a preference for curious chameleons as frontline fundraisers over posturing peacocks, and creating management incentives and metrics that encourage everyone to forge partnerships of shared purpose rather than closing gifts by year's end.

- Stewardship and donor relations professionals committed to dialogic approaches that encourage donors to share their perceptions of the institution and to suggest how the institution can be more accountable and responsive to them, as well as provide experiences for them to see and experience the differences they are making.

- Annual giving officers engaging donors in less formulaic ways (as developed by those in the annual fund consulting industry, who boast of improving annual results but do not mention the donor attrition and donor loss they have caused) and taking pains to ask alma mater (nourishing mother) questions (e.g., "Are you still paying off student debt?" "Which social cause is of greatest interest to you?" or "What has been your greatest personal and professional achievement since graduating?").

- Prospect researchers looking for evidence of the animating passions of prospects so that institutional representatives can engage them in ways that cause them to feel valued as human beings and potential partners in some greater cause or purpose.

- Alumni relations professionals seeking to understand how the lives of various generations of alumni were shaped, what they are trying to do with their lives, what they talk about at the dinner table, and what gives them hope and what keeps them awake at night – not just what campus events they want to attend or what sections of the alumni magazine they read most often.

- Writers and communicators reaching out to external constituents at every opportunity not just to write articles but to engage in research, not just to seek testimonials about the institution but to seek testimony about what drives conscientious people to give of themselves in service to a greater societal good, and not just feature donors but feature inspiring doers in all walks of life.

As this litany (incomplete as it is) suggests, listening, understanding, empathizing, and responding accordingly begin with an attitude that is converted to a goal, then backed up by sustained commitment.

To become better listening institutions – and therefore more strategic, adaptive, responsive, and relevant – leaders must do more than give lip service to the concept; they must "put teeth" into it and create the means for external constituents to see the difference. Presidents can put teeth in their pledge to listen by:

- Requiring evidence of objective listening and appropriate responsiveness in performance reviews of relevant officials.

- Creating frequent, high-level strategy sessions in which external scans are reviewed, responsive strategies are formulated, and/or the effectiveness of those strategies are reviewed.

- Creating the means within advancement operations and among institutional leaders to share information being regularly gathered – including summaries of donors' reactions to annual giving calls and polls, results of alumni surveys, synthesis of contact reports from donor meetings, constituent complaints lodged in any part of the organization, and reactions to the vetting of plans, white papers, and/or proposals with external constituents.

Presidents can cause external constituents to see the difference by:

- Giving speeches and providing reports that not only deal with institutional achievements but specific plans and aspirations to improve performance in select areas.

- Trusting external constituents with real information about real problems encountered.

Make them a partner

- Demonstrating how the institution engages in constant problem-solving not just endless self-promotion.

- Creating an environment where internal and external constituents feel safe in voicing concerns, proposing ways to improve, and showing that the institution understands that complaints come from caring, discerning people, not just chronic naysayers.

- Notifying key constituents of pending difficulties, controversies, and crises before they become the subject of media attention or constituent complaints.

The next level of integrating external evidence into the organizational life of an institution would be in discipline of creating agendas for meetings of the board, the president's executive team, councils of deans and other academic officials, and advancement meetings. Without such commitment from the top, and the living out of that commitment, advancement operations can devolve into any number of sub-optimizing postures, including:

- Ignoring external concerns or trying to counteract them with more promotional materials (like speaking louder when a person with perfect hearing simply cannot understand).

- Being receptive to constituent concerns but having no way to resolve them, thereby revealing the relative lack of importance the board and president assign to the advancement function and those it serves – and/or the fact that the president and the board see external relations as a one-way street: "We preach and promote; you give and praise."

- Creating environments where the administration can be seemingly blind-sided by accumulating constituent frustrations that cause donors and other external constituents to give less or stop giving – which then is blamed on substandard performance of advancement.

John Kenneth Galbraith described a revolution as "the kicking down of an already rotted door." The slow rot of various constituent doors has been ignored by too many institutions for too long and led, if not to a revolution, to a very sobering set of circumstances, including a 30-year decline of alumni giving, a significant loss of individual giving, an erosion of constituent affinity, and other trends that will be difficult to reverse. Yet, any recognition at the top and any willingness to listen better and respond more earnestly can begin the process of stemming if not reversing these trends. If this can be achieved, we can think about what advancement could achieve in a new, more hopeful light.

Advancement leaders can adapt to new philanthropic realities by thinking more about the key functions their organizations must perform rather than by specialty or donor segment.

The right side of the following chart reveals only some of the traditional specializations. In most organizations, there are many more including communications, prospect research, gift processing, event planning, and so on. The more boxes there are the greater the probability of losing sight of key functions.

By Function

- Mission Advancement
- VP Constituent Relations
- Constituent Research & Communication
- Volunteer Recruitment and Management
- Donor Retention
- Donor Acquisition

By Specialization

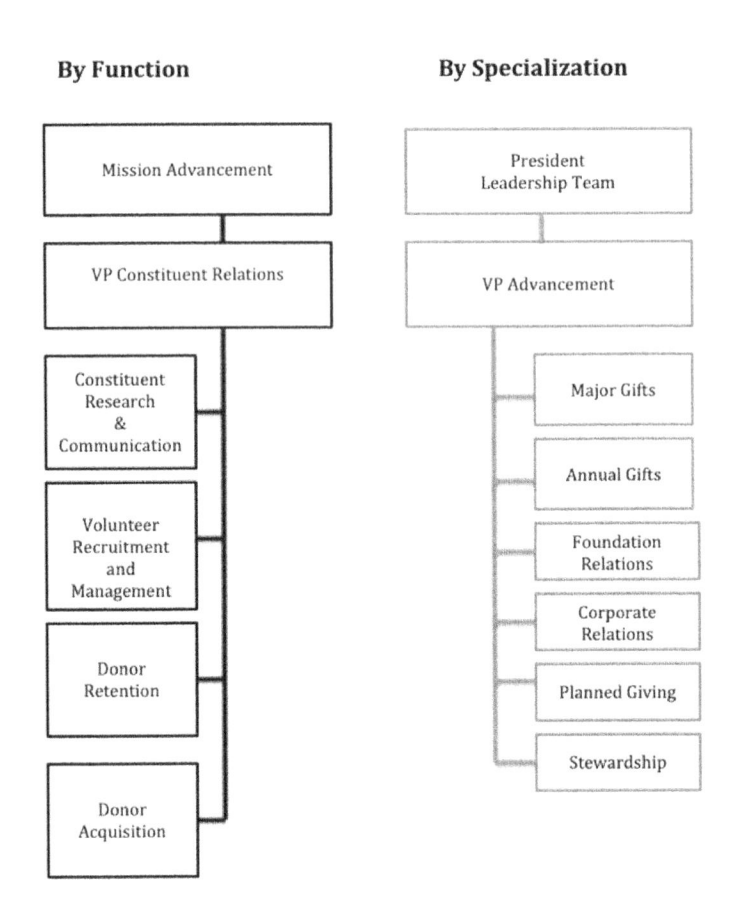

- President Leadership Team
- VP Advancement
  - Major Gifts
  - Annual Gifts
  - Foundation Relations
  - Corporate Relations
  - Planned Giving
  - Stewardship

Coordinating so many areas of expertise, nevermind managing egos that cause some practitioners to resist the broadening of their scope or the need to collaborate with others, can easily become a reactive function that diverts organizations from their more important strategic functions. Before we address how to build and manage a more functional organization, let us first make the case for the most important functions in which to focus.

Mission Advancement

The simple fact of the matter is that most presidents and their leadership teams focus much more of their effort on day-to-day administration rather than mission advancement milestones, often in the mistaken belief that energetic attentiveness to the former produces the latter. It doesn't. Just as we have learned the myth of multi-tasking – the more tasks we attempt the less well we do at each – so do we learn the depletive impact of adding more programs and services to bigger, seemingly more impressive organizations – or adding more people in response to growing market demands; the more we add, the more we sacrifice quality and key functionality. In a world where donors and other key constituents are increasingly concerned about the viability of educational institutions and more skeptical of giving to them lest they perpetuate dysfunction, institutional leaders must take greater pains to demonstrate how adept they are at managing current resources for optimal operational efficiency (as well as how secure and adaptive their institutions are) and to begin productive discussion as to how additional resources can add value and generate a greater societal return. They have to stop asking donors to give for the general good they have done and start asking donors to invest in the tangible good they could do. This will require more attention to mission outcome and less to administrative processes.

JAMES M. LANGLEY

Constituent Relations

This nomenclature seems better at capturing the essence of the role better than advancement, external relations, or development. Why? If we have lost over 20 million donors in the past two decades, does it not make eminent sense to place a higher premium on keeping the ones we have? Otherwise, we go looking for their replacements in a shrinking pool. Further, we know the retained donor is the more likely, most productive source of continued support, major gifts, and estate gifts. Consider:

- Donors retained year-over-year at the same level of giving serve as living endowments; those who give $1,000 a year provide the payout equivalent of a $25,000 endowment.

- Donors who give or pledge $1 million or more in any given year have given to the same organization for 15 years on average.

- Donors most likely to leave sizable estate gifts are either highly satisfied major gift donors and/or loyal annual donors of 20 years or more.

This tells us the best way to secure and sustain the most support has far more to do with being true to current donors than acquiring new ones. Yet, most advancement operations are much too oriented to new donor acquisition than donor retention – which explains the 13% decline in giving households in the U.S. in the past 20 years and increasing loss of trust in institutions.

At least 80% of what most institutions raise in any given year or in any given campaign comes from those who are giving or have given in recent years. It can be even higher if more institutions expend more effort on reinforcing the support they have rather than chasing seemingly larger but far more remote possibilities.

Constituent Research and Communication

Achieving the aforementioned purposes requires adopting classical marketing principles or simply placing more emphasis on:

- First, listening more closely to those who are already giving, including asking why they gave their first gift (which, surprisingly enough, is an invaluable insight missing from the vast majority of donor records) and exploring ways that the institution can better satisfy their deepest altruistic aspirations.

- Second, searching for new donors and doers whose altruistic aspirations align with the capabilities of the institutions and the ambitions of its initiative champions so that partnerships of shared purpose can be brokered with them.

- Third, making sure that the totality of altruistic aspirations being pursued under the aegis of the institution correspond to the larger needs, current or emerging, of community and society.

- Fourth, communicating in such a way to validate and deepen commitments made by donors and current constituents and to selectively attract new constituents to the institutions' portals of purpose.

As commonsensical as this all seems, the mindsets that underpin it and the approaches that flow from it are still relatively rare. Too many institutions continue to communicate in broad boastful ways, to "spray and pray," and to seek to mesmerize the masses rather than satisfy the discerning minds of current and prospective investors. The result is a colossal waste of their time, talent, and treasure. Efficiency is often measured using the roughest calculations: how much money we raised vs. how much we spent to raise it. Yet, a closer look at the activities and devices used to raise money, directly and indirectly, we see:

- Astonishingly expensive campaign launch events populated largely by staff and institutional insiders, including board members, and those who attend virtually every event offered.

- Pallets piled high with dust-gathering four-color brochures that proved obsolete or ineffective from the very outset.

- Increasing investments in larger numbers of higher-paid fundraisers who can't secure appointments with the majority of prospects in their portfolio and, when they do, struggle to secure the second appointment.

- Cases for support written in splendid institutional isolation then sprung on uninvolved prospects who say, "I don't see my purposes and values reflected in this," or "I was hoping to see a plan, not just a piece of literature."

- Website information (when tested with the alumni after the fact) is viewed as over-stated and/or irrelevant to their needs and interests.

- Videos of lots of people bouncing around offering often generic thanks to generic donors but leaving too few actual donors feeling genuinely thanked for their gift and still wondering about the impact of their investment.

- A calendar of events that crushes their planners but does little to attract key donors or prospects or, if they do, does little to cause them to become more committed to the institution.

In these, and many other ways, too many institutions confuse correlation with causation, assuming whatever they do in the name of fundraising actually causes people to give or give more, rather than verifying and measuring causal linkages. Those who take the time to test causality will conclude that too much of the fundraising industry has taken far too much credit for what it does and given too little credit to donors for what they do, sometimes despite what we do. One way of testing the accuracy of that statement is through the lens of giving in support of political candidates. People give to political campaigns because they believe in the candidate, not because they are asked a thousand times. They give to candidates who speak most authentically and closely to their values and who stand up for what they think is most important, not because they have produced the slickest campaign ads. They give because they are civically oriented, not because someone lectured them on the importance of voting. They give because they hope and pray that the candidate will make a significant sustainable difference in building a better society – and forgive the campaign for the rest, including the onslaught of often vacuous, manipulative solicitations.

Volunteer Recruitment and Management

Ample amounts of data show that greater attention to this function produces, among other things, improved donor retention and more significant, sustainable fundraising results. Volunteers give ten times more than passive donors over the course of their giving lives and twice as much each year, which suggests the importance of showing people how they can lend their time and talent (not just hounding them for their money) and how, with more energetic and adept attention to these functions, administrators could build stronger cultures and more relevant institutions.

Donor Retention

No function in an advancement operation is more important. This is not to say that the office of stewardship and/or the office of donor relations are more important than other

The Future of Fundraising

offices. Perhaps the most important, least understood fundraising truth is that you don't raise more money year over year by converting more prospects into donors but by converting more current donors into deeper believers with every passing year. Organizations that retain AND increase the confidence of their current donors year over year will always outstrip those that focus only on raising the most dollars from new donors in any given year. If presidents and boards could grasp this one point, they would stop asking fundraisers, "Why aren't you bringing in more dollars this year?" and start asking themselves and their senior administrative team, "Why didn't we inspire more of our donors to have more confidence in our greater long-term potential?" This we know: if they don't change this dynamic, their institutions will experience a greater sub-optimization of their donors giving potential, higher rates of donor attrition, and a higher churn rate of their most capable and conscientious fundraisers.

Donor retention, as a function, should command most of the time and talent of any advancement operation, if not much of the attention of the larger institution. First let's explore why the function is so important and then how it can be strengthened by greater collaboration with advancement functions and with a greater shared commitment across the institution.

Donor retention is important because:

- A retained donor is evidence of donor satisfaction.

- Donor satisfaction builds social capital which is an extremely important factor in creating a more favorable fundraising climate.

- The longer donors are retained the greater the probability of their continued giving (and thereby acting like a living endowment), of giving more (especially if their means increase), and of giving of their estate – or any combination thereof.

- Current and recently lapsed donors will provide at least 80% of future support, whether it is in the next year or the next five years.

- The U.S. and American higher education institutions that have been losing donors are likely to continue to do so without learning why and increasing counter-active measures.

Donor retention can be strengthened if advancement operations adopt it as their single most important objective. This, in turn, will cause them to:

- Listen more closely and more regularly with donors and with higher degrees of emotional intelligence.

- Gather more information from donors though all available channels (e.g., feedback on annual giving calls, what gift officers are learning from their interactions with donors, any concerns or complaints lodged by donors, donor attendance at key events, etc.).

- Gather more information in more systematic and scientific ways, including requiring advancement professionals to administer spot polls, discovery interviews or qualification visits, and/or telephonic interactions in a consistent fashion.

- Create polling questions and forensic interviews by calling upon marketing expertise on how to best frame questions to ensure that the responses are honest and objective.

- Train staff in the art and science of administering interviews in objective ways, in putting donors at ease, asking questions that cause donors to reveal their innermost hopes and concerns, and listening to their answers, and responding to them in more emotionally astute ways.

- Analyze and synthesize research and information gathering to gain greater insight into individual donor motivation as well as to pick up on shifting patterns in giving behaviors and preferences.

- Determine which fundraising strategies and tactics may yield short-term results but may increase the potential for higher donor attrition.

The efforts of advancement operations can be greatly enhanced in environments where leaders place a high premium on donor accountability and donor satisfaction. Leaders in such environments understand the importance of:

- Creating expedited review processes for gift proposals to ensure that they are reasonable, that the amount requested will cover the necessary additional costs, and that the institution will be able to deliver on any real and implied promises within.

- Converting carefully framed proposals into effective gift agreements that will allow their institutions to manage if not exceed donor expectations and avoid any potential misunderstandings, even with turnover in leadership and advancement positions.

- Having their boards understand the centrality of donor retention to institutional honor, accountability and reputation, and that they as boards and board members assist in the stewarding of donor groups (e.g., estate givers, loyal annual donors, major gift donors, etc.) as well as individual donors, particularly those that have given the largest amounts or given the longest number of years.

- Requiring the recipients of private support (including provosts, deans, and other academic and athletic officials) to demonstrate personal accountability and gratitude to donors, including authoring and personalizing regular impact reports.

- Creating an awareness of the role and importance of private giving in creating greater margins of institutional excellence that produce more significant sustainable societal gains.

It should be self-evident that the institutions that have and will sustain the highest levels of donor retention, and therefore enjoy all the benefits that flow from it, do not delegate stewardship and donor relations responsibilities down the chain of command to the lowest possible level but adopt a core ethic at the top of the organization and obligate all the beneficiaries of private funds to demonstrate responsible and responsive stewardship.

While the purpose of this chapter is to explain the most important functions that advancement operations must perform, the relative weighting of each, and the interdependence of the parts to the whole, in Chapter 6 we will explore in much greater detail how high functioning organizations strengthen donor retention.

Donor Acquisition

In this new world and new paradigm, donor acquisition plays a secondary functional role to donor retention and must be designed and approached to serve an increasingly strategic and sustainable purpose. And, in this new world, "donor acquisition" is a much more apt than "fundraising." The former more clearly describes the challenge and opportunity – to acquire donors according to their interests by demonstrating how an institution's capabilities align with their convictions, and how they can give through an institution for some greater societal gain. There's also opportunity to demonstrate how key people and teams in that institution are pursuing that goal, where they achieve success and when, through trial and error, they recognize the need to adjust and refine their approaches to create higher probabilities of success.

This is very different from generic fundraising that puts too much emphasis on giving and too little on outcomes, that asks donors to support institutional needs or institutional pursuits that do not correspond to donors' convictions, that ballyhoos dollars raised and speaks little of differences made, and that seeks to lather up prospects using too much supposedly promotional soap and too little substantive dialogue. The trouble with the concept of fundraising is that too many people and organizations took it literally and thought that's all there is to it – raising funds. What donors tell us in massive numbers, including the 20 million who have ceased supporting institutions, is that they are tired of being asked and tired of giving while getting so little back – or seeing so few real differences being made. Yes, there will always be those who, when offered a variety of giving options, will choose to give to a category like "greatest opportunities," but their probability of doing so will be greatly enhanced and facilitated by:

- Their personal appreciation for what the institution has done for them and their loved ones.

- Their feeling personally valued and respected by that institution.

- Being motivated by that institution's ambitions, which are specifically and clearly articulated.

- Believing in that institution's agency because of its ability to demonstrate significant sustainable societal gains from money invested in its specific, strategic pursuits.

- Seeing how many loyal adherents and highly satisfied donors it has retained through its good works.

In other words, while there will be those who do not choose to fund a specific strategic initiative, or to seek a particular portal of purpose, opting instead for the category that supports the entire institution, these individuals will be much more likely to do so and to give generously within their means, when they see the strategic specificity of its pursuits and its ability to convert investment into lasting impact. However, it should also be noted that such donors are also less likely to get involved, to invest larger amounts of their time, talent, and treasure as their means increase, and to give generous portions of their estates. Broad affirmation of general interest and casual, passive participation in institutional life will never, in the main, produce as much interest, energy, and investment as personal conviction and deep engagement.

Indeed, we would be better served if we thought of this function not as "donor acquisition" but as "constituent acquisition." This is because our best chances of acquiring new donors will be by demonstrating that we do not seek to acquire them just for their ability to give — as we did too often and too blatantly under the traditional fundraising model — but to acquire them first by showing how their convictions align with our capabilities, then to engage them by seeking out their talents, then secure their support by proposing partnerships of shared purposes, and then retain them by maintaining our dialogue with and by delivering on the promises we made. But, for now, let's leave it at "donor acquisition," so we don't upset too many cultural apple carts or cause too many decision-makers to fret that we may have forgotten that none of this is possible if we don't secure more private support.

This proposed model, with its emphasis on collaborating to perform key functions and thereby build more productive advancement cultures, promises to achieve another extremely important purpose – the retention of high achieving staff –

and to solve the riddle plaguing so many advancement operations – the extremely short average tenure (14-17 months) of fundraisers. Far more attention has been paid to fundraiser attrition than donor attrition – and no end of solutions have been discussed, including:

- More financial and nonfinancial incentives
- More training or coaching
- More personalized oversight
- Hiring those without direct experience but who possess similar skills
- Teambuilding exercises
- Flexible hours and work environments
- More realistic expectations, including smaller prospect portfolios

While all of these are worthy of consideration, the simple fact is that most organizations lose donors and fundraisers for essentially the same reasons. No donor woke up one morning and said, "I just want to give away money." No effective fundraiser woke up one day and said, "I just want to raise money." Both put some greater purpose first, then accepted the responsibility for its higher realization. That's why organizations that best define purpose, and where private support can make the greatest and most lasting impact, do the best job of attracting and retaining both. Further, as more and more donors protect themselves against the "schmooze and ambush" approach to fundraising and demonstrate less and less interest in responding to broad institutional requests, more and more astute fundraisers pick up and report these changing realities and urge higher ups to provide them with new concepts that will correspond to donors' interests. All too often this feedback is ignored or interpreted as excuse-making.

As the disparities between institutional ambitions and donor interest widens, even highly skilled fundraisers find themselves struggling to do both. Institutions that fail to hear and respond to field intelligence supplied by fundraisers compound the problem by imposing more rigorous metrics on those fundraisers believing that the real problem is a lack of focus and application. The more fundraisers are tasked to produce the unrealistic, the more likely some are to create the appearance of success by over-stating their efforts and accomplishments, and the more likely others are to ask donors for lesser amounts than they might give with more time and substantive dialogue afforded them, and still others are likely to look for work elsewhere. The more removed an institution grows from changing philanthropic behaviors (which can be achieved by simply standing still and engaging in the same fundraising practices over and over), the more dysfunction it and its fundraising operation becomes. It is stuck in time (with false or increasingly untrue assumptions) and in its organizational boxes where some practitioner may be doing remarkably well with their specialties under the circumstances but far less well than they could if they worked together to advance core functions.

In many operations, the emphasis on raising new dollars is so overstated and the need to retain donors is so understated — and the corresponding turnover of fundraisers is so great — that the only way to turn it around is through this nine-step plan, which advises advancement leaders to respond to the loss of each fundraiser by:

1. Replacing her/him with a donor relations specialist (DRS).

2. Assigning the prospect portfolio of the former fundraiser to the new DRS.

3. Encouraging and enabling the DRS to deepen the relationships of current donors by providing customized concierge services.

4. Asking the DRS to develop personalized acquisition strategies for new donors by researching and matching their deepest convictions with the organization's most exquisite competencies, making sure that all outreach to new donors is brokered by content experts, not traditional fundraisers.

5. Training content experts how to engage and involve new prospects, according to their talents and convictions.

6. Not soliciting the recently engaged for one year.

7. Repeating the process every time any fundraiser leaves.

8. Noting how fundraising results improve.

9. Hiring former fundraisers, if they run out of DRS candidates, and observing how much longer they stay now that they have more realistic and rewarding duties.

Indeed, this is the transition plan from the traditional "stacked box" organization built on individual specialties to the functional model – which proves more functional, sustainable, and enjoyable for everyone involved, including donors and fundraisers.

Many of the most accomplished advancement leaders have been striving and, in many cases, succeeding in making the specialized model more functional without explicitly adopting the proposed "by function" model. Some ask if they should actually recruit, hire, and manage their staff according to function titles rather than specialty titles. Yet, the "by function" model does not argue for the elimination of all specialization; it seeks to reduce if not obviate specialists pursuing lesser specialty goals while large functional ones go ignored or ill-attended. For example, imagine how differently many advancement organizations would operate if they:

- Rank-ordered their best prospects irrespective of whether they were individual, foundations, corporations, or organizations, and assigned its best people, irrespective of specialty, to optimize the potential of those prospects in rank order; in such instances, the head of corporate relations might have 35 corporate prospects and 25 individual ones (perhaps with strong corporate identities) while the head of foundation relations might have 31 foundations and 52 individual prospects (perhaps those whose giving interests map against those giving propensities of foundations), and an individual gift officer had a blend of all three because he or she had the best insight into the interests and motivations of each prospect.

- Viewed their best planned giving opportunities through a broader lens — meaning, no cajoling the elderly to think about the possibility but working with those who were on the most likely tracks to become estate givers, including loyal donors who have given for 20 years of more, highly satisfied donors who had given two or three major gifts, and long-serving volunteers; in such circumstances the head of the annual fund, who knew the loyalist the best, would be working alongside major gift officers who knew major donors the best, as well as someone in stewardship and/or donor relations, an alumni relations representative, and others tasked with doing all they could to make those donors want to leave estate gifts to continue and extend the purposes that defined and animated their lives.

- Created a team to study donor attrition at any level, to search for any underlying reasons that may be causing it, and to intervene at the earliest opportunity to turn donor concerns or complaints into learning opportunities.

In such examples, we see there is always a need for specialists to act as experts and perform specialized tasks and to also always be team players in pursuit of larger opportunities. To better understand how this could work, let's look at a composite case study of actual best practice in a fictional setting.

The Future of Fundraising

The next chapter will take us inside the fictional Arkadelphia University to see how:

- Practices espoused thus far in this book play out in an "actual" setting.

- New opportunities are created when we discover more about the animating passions of our current donors.

- Customized engagement can heighten donor interest.

- Closer listening and personalized problem-solving leads to more successful gift closures.

- Collaboration, within advancement and between advancement and various academic and administrative officials, helps optimize the giving potential of our donors and prospects.

JAMES M. LANGLEY

CHAPTER 5
THE ESSENTIALITY OF COLLABORATION

Case Study

An adept researcher on the advancement staff at Arkadelphia University, while entering the latest gift from Ophelia Lemieux, thought she saw a pattern in her larger gifts – which were never that large. Ms. Lemieux had given small annual gifts for 18 years and the occasional modest gift for what seemed a variety of purposes – to the debate team, to the music department, to nursing, and to the Honors College. But upon closer look, the researcher began to wonder if the thread running through them was an underpinning belief in the power of experiential learning. The gift to the debate team had been to travel to the national semi-finals, the gift to the music department was to underwrite overseas performances for the student orchestra, the gift to nursing was a simulation lab, and the gift for the Honors College was for a program that paired those students with intellectually-challenged teenagers in the local community.

The researcher dug deeper, looking for Ms. Lemieux's giving elsewhere or other evidence of her deepest philanthropic propensities. The researcher discovered that Ms. Lemieux had given a series of smallish gifts to her alma mater, which seemed to suggest a similar pattern. The researcher called her counterpart at Ms. Lemieux's alma mater but found her reluctant to share any insight. While the other researcher said she was loath to share "confidential information," it was clear to the AU researcher that her counterpart had never attempted to put the pieces together.

The researcher then sought to identify the gift officers at AU who might have worked with Ms. Lemieux to gather their insights into her philanthropic motivations. To her amazement, no gift officer had been assigned to Ms. Lemieux because of the relatively modest amount of each gift. The AU researcher then called their long-serving stewardship director to see if she had any insight into Ms. Lemieux. The mere mention of the donor's name caused the stewardship director to wax rhapsodic. "Oh, Ophelia! She's so nice, so wise, so modest." The stewardship director described Ophelia as "a reactor" – someone who would give reactively to something she read in one of the University publications or heard about while attending campus events. If she liked what she heard or read, she sent in a gift in support. No one had ever solicited her. When Ophelia received an impact report from the stewardship office or a handwritten note from one of the recipients, she always wrote the stewardship office to say how much she appreciated learning how much students had benefited from "real life experiences." Bingo. The researcher's instincts had just been validated.

Before hanging up, the researcher asked the stewardship director, "Do you know why she started giving to AU, since she's not an alumnus?" There was a long pause before the stewardship director said, "I have no idea… but shouldn't we know that?"

The researcher now knew she was on to something. She began digging more. Though Ms. Lemieux lived in a modest house and engaged in no known extravagances, she had sold a hugely successful family business a decade ago and, based on the large number of subsequent stock purchases, turned those proceeds into a diverse investment portfolio. The researcher could find lots of evidence of stock purchases but no significant liquidations.

The researcher then called the new vice president for advancement, knowing exactly how to get his attention.

"I've got a very good prospect for you."

"Oh, great, who?"

"Ophelia Lemieux."

"Really," he replied, with a large dollop of skepticism in his voice. "Isn't she that nice old lady who has given a bunch of little gifts?"

"So far, but only because we may have missed the obvious."

"What do you mean?" he asked a bit defensively.

"She's never been managed as a prospect. She's given every gift without any prompting."

"Well, that's nice, but…"

"And it looks like she has considerable wealth."

The Future of Fundraising

"Doesn't she drive some sort of ancient Buick?"

"She's a classic philanthropist. She's living well under her means and giving away the margin – and there's a lot more she could give away, especially if we find the right initiative."

"Like what?"

"Something to do with experiential learning."

A sound thesis on Ms. Lemieux's philanthropic propensities had been formed. The best people in AU advancement knew that fundraising is all theory until the right idea, one that has a strong probability of resonating with a prospect's values and purposes, is presented in the right way at the right time by the right person. The team was struggling with a big, high-impact idea to put in front of Ms. Lemieux until the director of alumni affairs asked the dean of Arts and Sciences to speak to an alumni gathering in Little Rock.

"I've spent the last year listening to a lot of students, to a lot of alumni," said the dean, "and a lot of parents and a lot of employers."

"The good news," he continued, "is that all of them believe in the lasting value of the liberal arts. Students say they love the breadth of learning opportunities. The alumni say that we kept our promise, that we actually gave them a base of knowledge to last a lifetime. The parents say they know their children will work in an ever-changing economy and want to be able to adapt and prosper with change. Employers say that our graduates are among the most promotable.

"The bad news is that all say that we have a short-term problem. Students and parents worry about their debt load and what sort of job they will be able to land that will allow them to pay off that debt. Employers worry about the cost of training new employees, even the most promising ones, especially when their profit margins grow thin, and alumni tell us they would have been able to get the all-important first job if they had graduated with more practical skills.

"So, how obvious does it have to be before we realize that we must augment that traditional liberal arts with the liberal arts of the next century and interlace what the past has proven to be sound with what the future will demand with a host of practical opportunities? When do we begin to think of ourselves as a College of proven and practical arts?"

The alumni were applauding, and the alumni director, having been privy to a strategy session on Ophelia Lemieux, knew that a powerful partnering opportunity was unfolding, one that had the potential of putting an innovative doer in front of an impassioned donor.

Within days of the dean's talk, key members of the advancement team were meeting with him to translate his broad vision into an action plan, one that defined what could be done within existing resources and where private support would make a significant and lasting difference. Days later, they had identified several areas where a significant gift would be highly catalytic to the realization of the dean's vision of creating a College that melded the proven with the practical. They were:

THE FUTURE OF FUNDRAISING

1. The Dean's Innovation Fund, which would allow the dean to reward faculty and various department heads who proposed the most innovative ways of creating new experiential learning opportunities.

2. Student Incentive Awards, which would be given to students whose research merited presentation at national meetings, students who presented the most innovative ideas for augmenting their studies with practical opportunities, and student organizations that won the right to compete at national events but who could not afford the travel.

3. Alumni Distinguished Practitioner Awards, which would provide stipends to young, highly accomplished Arts & Sciences alumni to share practical learning opportunities with students, including acting as problem-solving teams in workplaces, conducting market research and field studies, and to help older workers identify and employ new technologies.

4. Project Arkansas, which would allow cross-disciplinary teams of students to meet with the CEOs and senior executives of the most successful companies in the state to learn about the skillsets that will be in greatest demand in the years ahead.

5. Adaptive Internships, which would provide prevailing wages for innovative internships with nonprofits, startup companies, and government.

This action plan was developed into a white paper, clearly marked "draft" so that it could be put in front of potential funders and partners and refined through honest give and take. Some put Ms. Lemieux on the top of that list while others expressed deep skepticism about her giving potential. Two frontline fundraisers said she was "small potatoes" and not worth the time. Another asserted, "If she were going to do anything meaningful, she would have done it by now."

The planned giving director weighed in saying, "Most of the planned gifts we get come from people like her – loyal, quiet, unassuming, and very modest in their lifestyle." When others remained unconvinced, he asserted, "She's the real deal. I'd bet on it."

The senior researcher, the director of research, and one of the most capable fundraisers agreed, dubbing her "Real Deal Ophelia" or RDO for short. The vice president, having listened to both sides, said, "Okay, we need an approach strategy." From then on, all team meetings focused on engineering personal, productive, and progressive interactions with Ms. Lemieux were labeled "RDO Sessions."

The question was how to begin that conversation and who should reach out to her. Some argued that it should be the president, despite the fact that he had no relationship with Ms. Lemieux, because his presence would lend weight to the initiative. Others argued for a combination of the president, the dean of A&S, and the vice president for advancement. Once again, the vice president listened to all sides before announcing, "It has to be the dean. By himself."

Some questioned if the dean, given his lack of fundraising experience, could go it alone. The vice president said, "The one who has the closest relationship with her is Ann (the stewardship director), but this meeting is about exploring an alignment of interests. The architect of the initiative has the best chance of achieving that. If she doesn't believe in him and what he is proposing, none of us will be able to compensate."

While some worried out loud about the risks associated with the proposed approach, the alumni director said, "I've seen the guy with alumni. He's thoughtful and genuine. No one will broker this idea better than him."

The dean, upon being asked to make direct contact with Ms. Lemieux, had a pang of self-doubt but came around with the encouragement of the vice president who kept counseling, "Just be yourself and let your conviction shine through."

The dean decided to call, rather than e-mail Ms. Lemieux and request an appointment with her. When she answered, he introduced himself and thanked her for her recent and previous gifts. "You seem to care a great deal about hands-on learning," he said.

"Well, yes, I do," she said. "It's nice of you to have noticed that."

"I've developed a plan to make that an integral part of the College," he said, "and would love to get your candid reaction to it."

"I don't know that I would have much to offer," she said.

"I see the thoughtfulness in your giving and know I would benefit from your advice. I'd be happy to pay you a visit – whenever it might be convenient."

There was a long pause. The dean not only felt his heart in his throat but heard it pounding in his ears — so loudly that he began to wonder if it could be heard on the other end of the line.

After what seemed like an eternity, she said, "Well, if you think it would be helpful."

The provost and president were briefed on the initiative and gave it their blessing. The president knew little about Ms. Lemieux and, because he sensed she was a minor prospect, was happy to delegate the opportunity to the dean.

Ms. Lemieux could not have been more gracious when the dean came to call. He presented her with a four-page draft of his plan explaining, "I've never done anything like this before, but I am absolutely convinced it needs to be done."

He took her through the plan, then asked for her candid critique.

"It strikes me as very sensible," she said. "How has your faculty reacted?"

That question and those that followed impressed the dean. Ms. Lemieux was wise to the ways of the world and to the inner workings of higher education. She knew that real change had to come from within and that cultures turn slowly.

"I don't believe in sweeping change," she said. "I think it is more about a thousand nudges, and you can't be the only one doing the nudging.

"The way you propose to use incentives is very smart," she said. "The question is how many people will actually respond to them."

The dean thanked her for her sound advice and said, "I hope we can turn this into an ongoing conversation."

She nodded and smiled slightly.

The dean promised to reflect on their discussion and to think more about building an internal consensus and other ways that the plan could be improved.

The dean, knowing the advancement team would be eager to hear how the meeting had gone, swung by the vice president's office when he returned to campus. The vice president asked his assistant to see if others on the leadership team would like to join him for the debrief with the dean.

Everyone was encouraged by the news. After all, she had taken the meeting, had listened carefully, and offered thoughtful advice. "What I find encouraging," said the AVP for development, "is the way she was advising you how to be successful. She wants this to work."

The annual fund director, having been briefed on the efforts to create an alignment of interest with Ms. Lemieux, went back through her annual gifts to see if he could find any additional clues. She had given $1,000 a year for 18 straight years, always on the last Friday in December, but no one had been able to budge her above that amount. Yet, in that search, he found an intriguing insight. In a telefund conversation six years earlier,

Ms. Lemieux had been complimentary of the student caller, told him how important it was to gain practical experience and how the family company (Lemieux Instruments) had become increasingly successful when it increased the number of student internships, and used the program to identify its most promising future employees. "We always looked for the broadly educated with specific, extensive practical experience," she said.

That tip, coupled with the dean's takeaways, made the vice president realize that they all would benefit from a more in-depth understanding of Lemieux Instruments (LI), especially what had allowed it to become more successful. He asked the head of research to not only develop a company profile but to see if she could find any articles about the company's ethos and operating principles. A couple of days later, she came back with a treasure trove of relevant information. Key among her finds were:

- LI had been founded by Ophelia's father, who was heralded throughout his career as a pioneer in "workplace innovation."

- Her father had attacked "the stacked box approach" reflected in most company's organizational charts. "There's no greater way to kill innovation than to hire a bunch of specialists, place them in a rigid hierarchy, house them in comfy little offices, and reward them only for their individual talent and individual performance."

- LI had fostered a high-level of internal communication by ensuring that every person in the organization, at every level, understood the company's priorities including growth strategies, strategic priorities, and current projects.

- LI built a round building with glassed in offices around the perimeter so employees could close the door and concentrate, when they needed to, but always "walk the ring" each day so they could familiarize themselves with the projects each person was working on. This was accomplished by requiring every person to place a list of current projects on their outer door so that it could be read by anyone walking the ring. Those project lists were expected to spell out the goals for each, the status of each, and any issues that the project leader may be ruminating about or struggling with.

- Anyone who saw the potential for collaboration, who thought they had something to contribute, or who simply had a question about a project being worked on by a colleague could request a "collaborative exploration appointment," which could be done at lunch, during the last hour of the day, or by appointment. Anyone could beg off from such a request on any given day if they were up against a deadline or dealing with an emergency, but pay raises were based on evidence of collaborations leading to improved internal communication, product design, or customer satisfaction.

- The inner ring of each floor was for group meetings, prototype displays (to invite reviews and suggestions), and the posting of communal messages, including upcoming meeting topics.

- LI had received an enormous amount of positive press in business magazines, often cited for its ability to put the breadth of cross-collaboration over the depth of highly specialized knowledge – yet excelled in a field that demanded mastery of technological specificity.

- Every employee was expected to know the 25 most significant (in terms of total value of goods purchased) and the 25 most loyal customers (based on the total number of years of having purchased LI products).

When the vice president read this briefing, he felt a rush of kinship with the company and a wave of affirmation because, in his own way, even without the benefit of a round building, he had worked diligently to create an advancement operation with a similar ethos.

The dean, after reading the briefing, understood why Ms. Lemieux had been able to ask such penetrating questions and what he would have to be more conscious about in communicating with her in the future – that they shared many of the same values.

The RDO team then discussed next steps. The dean said he wanted to spend time with his department chairs and to ask them to spend time with the faculty to see how the plan could be made more appealing to them. Weeks later, after those discussions had taken place, the dean learned that there was solid support for the overall concept, with the youngest faculty being the most enthusiastic. The department chairs said that many faculty were receptive to competing for grants from Deans Innovation Fund but advised that the awards "had to be large enough to make them want to compete and, if they were successful, to have a real impact." The dean asked the department chairs to sound out some of the more enthusiastic faculty about the kind of ideas they would like to put forward and what it would cost to launch them.

Meanwhile the alumni director began sounding out some of the most impressive A&S alumni about the Distinguished Practitioner Awards, while the vice president and director of corporate relations began meeting with employers, some of whom were alumni, to glean their reactions to Project Arkansas and the Adaptive Internship program.

In a few days, the dean was in receipt of four specific ideas from various faculty members, two of which estimated they needed $10,000 to implement their idea, while one suggested $25,000 and another $40,000.

The dean called Ms. Lemieux to brief her on the progress being made, including the fact that the overall concept was meeting with little faculty resistance, only some skepticism on the part of few, some detachment on the part of others, but varying degrees of enthusiasm from the remainder.

"That's encouraging," she said. "Would you like me to fund one of those faculty proposals?"

The question caught him completely off guard. He sputtered for a few seconds before recovering his bearing and saying,

"Thank you, Ophelia. But it's too early. I have to get the fundamentals in place before we ask anyone to support it."

The dean, when he reported the conversation later, was relieved to hear from the vice president that he had "done exactly the right thing."

The alumni director reported that the young, successful A&S alumni were very complimented by the outreach and thought the proposed initiative to be conceptually sound but questioned if there was adequate infrastructure in the College to launch and sustain the effort.

The vice president and corporate relations director received positive feedback, particularly on the issue of adaptive internships, but also stern advice including:

- "Don't launch until you have all your ducks in a row. There's been too much stopping and starting at AU in recent years."

- "We want one-stop shopping. We don't want to have to meet with four or five people to get something done."

- "Your internship program is outmoded. You're still trying to place students in big companies to be gofers rather than placing them in smaller companies and startups where they will have real responsibility."

- "If you say 'adaptive,' you need to mean it. It still sounds like you want 9-5, Monday through Friday jobs for one semester. That's not how we work. We want interns in the evenings, on weekends and when we need them. You have to adapt to our realities."

The dean realized how important it was to under-promise and over-deliver and to carefully phase in each aspect of the overall initiative. He decided the most important objectives to achieve in the short run were funding the best experiential ideas coming from the faculty and to generate more adaptive internships by working more closely with local businesses and/or A&S alumni.

Before requesting another meeting with Ophelia, the name she now insisted he use, to provide a very candid briefing on the status of the initiative, he engaged the RDO team. The dean said, "I know she will ask again, 'What can I do to help?' What should I say?" The vice president pointed out how important it was to get Ms. Lemieux more involved, so she could see the initiative's potential for herself before making a financial request. The best writer on staff stressed how important it was to be more conscious of, and employ words and concepts that would resonate with Ms. Lemieux and the ethos of Lemieux Instruments, in both oral and written briefings, and said she stood by to provide that assistance. The dean gladly and readily accepted her offer.

When the dean and Ophelia met, the meeting unfolded with remarkable ease. The dean could see the benefit of all the forethought that had been given to the meeting, including word choice and affirming their shared values. He noted how often she used the word "we" as she imagined how the initiative would unfold. And, yes, she asked again, "How can I help?" The dean responded by asking her to come to a meeting on campus in which he, A&S faculty, the director of the Career Planning, and several members of Advancement would be reviewing the current slate of experiential opportunities available to students and how they might be augmented in the next two semesters. He told her they would also be hearing directly from students who had been engaged in various experiential learning opportunities. Ophelia, delighted to be offered such a meaty opportunity, eagerly accepted.

The dean and the vice president, in their debrief meeting, landed on one key outcome for the meeting, which they expressed in almost exactly the same way. "This is our opportunity to show her what is possible, not just tell her, to show her how we think, how we collaborate, and how determined we are to make a meaningful difference."

The vice president appointed his stewardship director to serve as Ophelia's point of contact before the meeting and act as concierge when she arrived on campus. While some members of the fundraising staff clamored for that role, the VP reasoned that the stewardship director should get the nod because:

1. She'd had the most interaction with the prospect.
2. It was a stewardship function.

The stewardship director called Ophelia three times before the campus meeting. The first was to take her through the outline of the meeting, which she had sent in advance of the call, to see if she would be able to attend the entire meeting and to see if she would like to do anything else on campus, including spend time with the President. Ophelia declined the opportunity to meet with the President saying, "I'm sure he has bigger fish to fry," but adding, "It would be wonderful if I could see Amanda Johnson."

Amanda was the administrative assistant in the Events office, the person who staffed the reception table at virtually every major event. It seemed that Amanda had always greeted Ophelia so warmly and made her feel so at home. Amanda also read the campus newspaper and kept up on the latest gifts, so she was always able to thank Ophelia for the latest act of generosity. "She always made me feel like it was the most important gift in the world," said Ophelia, "and she was so attentive, ushering me about and always making sure I got a nice seat at every event."

The next time the stewardship director called was to take her through the event logistics, including where to park, how to display the parking pass, the name of the student who would greet her in the parking lot and take her to the meeting, how she would be greeted and introduced by the dean, and the fact that she should feel free to participate fully in the meeting discussion.

The third call was the evening before to make sure Ophelia had everything she needed. Ophelia, chagrined to reveal that she had spilled coffee all over her parking pass, asked if another might be made available. "The student greeting you will have it," said the stewardship director.

The day unfolded almost perfectly. Ophelia was delighted to be escorted by such a kind and impressive student, to be greeted so affectionately when she entered the building by Amanda, to be welcomed so warmly and introduced so generously by the dean, and to take part in such a weighty discussion with so many smart and well-intended professionals. By day's end, she felt quite privileged to have been a part of it all.

She was escorted back to her car by the stewardship director, who said, "We're so fortunate to have you as a part of our community. I'm embarrassed to say that I don't know how or why you first became involved with AU."

"Oh, it was years and years ago," she said. "I had been shopping in the outlet mall and was walking back to my car when I saw an older woman, using a walker, trying to negotiate a curb in the parking lot. One wheel plunked down hard and threw her completely off balance, and she fell down hard. I was so concerned about how hard she had fallen and rushed over to her. Before I could get there, a young man rushed to her side. He was very careful in the way he got her to straighten out, so soothing in the way he attended to her, asking her name and if she was feeling any pain as he held her hand. He insisted that she not try to get up. He continued to hold her hand as he somehow dialed his cell phone with the other. He seemed to know just what to do and who to call. I stayed with him and her until some people came in an ambulance… what do you call them?"

"EMT's," the stewardship director guessed.

"Yes, that was it. After they had taken care of her and helped her back up, I told the young man how impressed I was with his manner and asked him how it was that he knew just what to do. He told me he was a nursing student at AU and that he was in his senior year and had been working in an assisted living center. I sent in a donation to the nursing school and started receiving a newsletter about campus events. I wondered if you might have other students as impressive as that young man ... and one thing led to the other."

Within two days of the meeting, the dean received a handwritten note from Ophelia thanking him for the invitation, telling him how appreciative she was to be a part of the interaction and how impressed she was by the caliber of the people on his team.

The dean concluded that he needed time to synthesize all the advice and information he had received in recent months before re-engaging Ophelia and other prospects. But he wrote her a handwritten note thanking her for her attendance and letting her know he would be getting back to her in about two weeks. In further discussion with the Advancement team and others, he decided that it was important to establish the most attainable short-term objectives and to continue to provide the context of the overarching initiative and the goal of becoming a College of proven and practical arts. When he had his thoughts worked out, he asked for another RDO session with the Advancement team before asking for another meeting with Ophelia. Foremost on the dean's mind was, "Should I put out a number if she asks what she can do?"

If Ophelia were to give, the dean felt the best use of her funds would be to underwrite the most promising proposals submitted by the department heads and faculty.

"I'd love to be able to build an endowment for the Dean's Innovation Fund," he said, "but I could make good use of $85,000 right now." That amount was very close to Ophelia's total giving to date and would, therefore, be her largest gift by a wide margin.

"Is she ready to step up that much?" asked the senior fundraiser.

"Maybe we should ask for half," the vice president mused.

Everyone agreed that the time was right to ask, for no one wanted to miss an opportunity by asking for too much or too little.

"I bet she offers a much smaller amount," said the stewardship director.

"I'd ask for the full amount," said the planned giving director. "The number is real, and she wants to help … but she may not know how."

"What does that mean?" asked the dean.

"From all we can tell, she has considerable wealth and lots of appreciated assets but most of it is illiquid. She may not know how to liquidate assets or use illiquid assets to create a trust," the planned giving director explained.

"How could someone with that much money *not* know how to do those things?" the dean asked.

"Oh, it's not unusual," the planned giving director said. "There are lots of people who know how to make money and manage money who don't have a clue about their charitable giving options."

"Should you go with me?" the dean asked the planned giving director.

"Not this time," he said. "If she's prepared to give it outright and has sufficient liquidity to do so, you don't need me. If she doesn't, I can come in the next time."

"Should I ask for more than $85,000? How about $100,000?" the dean asked.

The vice president shook his head. "No, only ask her for what is real, no padding. We need to establish that we're working with her as a partner on this initiative, not trying to extract a particular amount."

With the blessing of all, the dean secured another meeting with Ophelia in which he laid out his short-term objectives while quick to remind her that he was still adamant about his long-term goal. As everyone predicted, she asked how she might help. The dean laid out his rationale for funding the most promising faculty proposals which, he said, "would come to $85,000."

Ophelia looked down. There was a long pause. The dean had been coached "to not rush into the silence," no matter how long or how awkward, and to not retreat from the number because it was real and essential to moving his initiative forward.

"I'd like to be able to do that," said Ophelia, seeming to choose each word deliberately. "But I'm not sure I can."

"I'm not here to press you for an answer," the dean said, "just share what we are trying to accomplish."

"Oh, I understand," said Ophelia, "and I think it's very important. It's something I'd like to do."

When the dean reported back to the RDO team, the planned giving director said, "I thought that might be the case. She sees herself living on fixed income."

"Well, the wolves aren't exactly at her door," said the senior fundraiser.

"She sees herself as a steward of family assets and wants to pass them on to her children. My guess is that she's trying to maintain a certain corpus, probably around $75 million …"

"Really!" said the dean. "Are you sure? That sounds awfully high."

"I'd say it's really close," said the planned giving director. "I think she's living on about half earnings from interest bearing assets and giving the rest away."

"How would you know that?" asked the stewardship director.

The Future of Fundraising

"I've seen it before. Someone with significant wealth and strong philanthropic instincts but locked into a set of financial assumptions."

"So, what do we do?" asked the dean.

"Let me see if I can spend some time with her," said the planned giving director.

"Should I go with you?" asked the dean.

"I don't think so. But I will drop your name."

The planned giving direction reached Ms. Lemieux on the phone, referring to the last conversation with the dean. "I understand that you're interested in helping fund the dean's experiential education initiative," he said.

"Yes, very much," said Ophelia, "but I'm afraid most of my wealth is ... on paper."

"Do you mean stocks and bonds?" he asked.

"Yes, and they go up and down, which makes it hard to figure out how much I'll have to live on and to help others."

"Did you know that you have certain vehicles available to you that will allow you to put your money in a trust for charitable purposes and to draw a guaranteed rate of interest?"

"Why, no."

"And in the process reduce your taxes."

"Do you work for AU?"

"Yes, I'm the director of planned giving. I'd love to take you through some of the options you have to see which might work best for you."

"Well, if you work for AU, I suppose that would be fine."

When the planned giving director met with Ophelia, he found her a quick study and one who seemed quite delighted to learn about the options and advantages that charitable giving provided her. The planned giving director knew he was not there simply to seize on her enthusiasm to close a gift but to build trust. He urged her to seek independent corroboration and advice from her financial advisor and/or lawyer. If she preferred, he said, he would be happy to recommend several very capable independent financial advisors.

"It's so funny," Ophelia said, "but I have never talked to my accountant about this."

In fact, her financial advisor was quite delighted to learn that she wanted to explore those options. He had assumed, having worked with her for many years, that she was nominally philanthropic and more concerned with wealth retention. He was eager to take her through the various trust options available to her and the attendant, tax advantages, while she took utter delight in her newfound philanthropic power.

About a week later, the dean took a call from Ophelia.

"I can do it," she said. "The $85,000."

The Future of Fundraising

Before he could express his delight, she said, "And I'm going to give the same amount next year."

The dean was beside himself with delight and overwhelmed with gratitude.

"I've established a lead trust!" she said. While the dean wasn't quite sure what that meant, he could hear how perfectly delighted she was.

The news of her gift created a ripple of ecstasy across the university, as well as in the College and throughout the Advancement operation. The president immediately penned a handwritten note, as did the dean and vice president. The stewardship director called Ophelia to ask how she would like her gift to be announced.

"I don't want any fuss made about me, but I would like a statement expressing how important I think this initiative is and how consistent it is with my father's philosophy."

The story doesn't end here. The dean embraced Ophelia not only as a generous donor but as a trusted advisor. He reviewed his plans with her, asked her to attend various meetings, and gave her candid assessments of what was working, where he was struggling, what he was learning from the process, and what refinements he was making along the way.

Sixteen months after her first investment, she announced that she was giving $100,000 a year to the Dean's Innovation Fund for the next five years and leaving a $2 million endowment through her estate.

Nor does the story end there. A little more than three years later, she gave another $500,000 for student incentive awards and increased the size of her estate commitment by creating another $3 million endowment, the earnings from which could be "expended at the dean's discretion."

Lessons Learned

The story of Ophelia Lemieux and Arkadelphia University is an amalgam of many real major gifts that have unfolded in similar ways across many institutions of higher learning. Those who have worked in reasonably high-functioning cultures will see many similarities in their own experiences. Those who have worked or are working in less healthy cultures may wish they had or could be involved in more such experiences. Those in low functioning cultures may be surprised to learn not only how higher functioning cultures work but why such cultures will consistently raise far more money over time.

Arkadelphia University is a fictional university. It is not an example of a prestigious college or university with all sorts of advantages that redound to its fundraising capabilities. It is an example of a strong regional university that has had a significant regional impact. Yet, it is an example of how an institution can inspire and sustain the confidence of a significant number of philanthropic investors by going about its business in the right way.

Why is AU an example of "the right way?" Let's explore that at several important levels.

The Right Outlook: Cherry Picking vs. Cultivating Cherry Orchards

First, throughout the interactions with Ophelia Lemieux, AU professionals focused on creating a strong alignment of interests between the donor's values and the institution's capabilities. They did not seek to get a gift as soon as possible – in the name of meeting individual metrics or annual fundraising totals – but to create a stronger community of shared purposes. In other words, they were far more focused on creating the conditions that would foster sustainable philanthropy than on short-term fundraising objectives. Operations that obsess about short-term results are always scrambling to meet them. That's the trouble with a "cherry picking" mentality. Operations that strike the right balance between long-, mid-, and short-term objectives grow cherry orchards that yield bountiful harvests over time.

Second, the emphasis at AU on achieving an alignment of interest with their prospects, rather than just asking them to give to AU for what AU wanted, empowered the research director, at the beginning of the case study, to not just enter the latest gift from Ms. Lemieux but to ask herself, "How does this give us more insight into her philanthropic propensities?" and to use that information to instigate a process that would lead to a more satisfying and productive relationship between the donor and the University.

Third, the insight into Ms. Lemieux's philanthropic motivation then led the advancement team in pursuit of the person at AU with the capability of satisfying her interests. Because of the openness within AU advancement and the fact that the VP had established larger imperatives (e.g., that fundraising isn't about getting people to do what we want but to find ways of advancing together), the alumni director was able to identify the dean whose vision and determination made him an ideal partner for Ms. Lemieux. This would not have happened in a stove-piped, specialized, non-communicative culture. In such operations, people like research directors are expected to behave tactically (e.g., build donor profiles) rather that to be attuned and responsive to the psychology of donors. In such operations, alumni directors would not have known, nor been encouraged, to look for Ms. Lemieux's potential partnership within AU.

It is also important to note that the culture at AU was not merely to satisfy the whims of various donors, which is the flipside of fundraising solely for institutional purposes. The culture at AU was such that the players in this story knew there was no point going forward with Ms. Lemieux if her interests did not correspond to a strategic initiative.

The Right Approach to Teamwork

Look at the number of individuals that played a vital role in winning and sustaining Ms. Lemieux's support:

- Administrative assistant
- Alumni director
- Annual Fund director

The Future of Fundraising

- Career Planning director
- Corporate Relations director
- Dean
- Department heads
- Faculty
- Planned Giving director
- President
- Researcher
- Fundraisers
- Staff writer
- Stewardship director
- Students, past and present
- Telefund caller
- Vice President

In a good gift example, all of these are run by the Gift Officer

And this list probably understates the number of people involved when one considers those working behind the scenes. In addition, in this case study we see the willingness of individual players to contribute to the whole. Some provided invaluable support from behind the scenes, some through direct interaction with the donor. Each was willing do what was best for that donor under those circumstances. The fundraisers, for instance, played more of strategic support roles, deferring to those who had stronger personal relations with the donors and those who were most capable of articulating the greater purposes of the proposed initiative. The fundraisers, to their great credit and professionalism, did not assert, "We're the experts. We should handle this and everyone else should stay out of our business." In fact, the assertion of individual expertise as being greater than the capabilities of the team can be highly undermining of organizational efficiency. When leaders recruit and hire talent on the basis of their stand-alone expertise and allow them to operate as lone wolves, they miss or fail to optimize the potential of the Ms. Lemieux's of the world and fail to create the conditions that will allow organizations to retain large numbers of donors long enough to reach their full philanthropic maturity. Yes, as is the case with all teams, there are times when one person should carry the ball, and some professionals who are better equipped to do so but all ball carriers achieve greater results when they allow themselves to be assisted by teammates and when they distinguish when it should be their turn and when it should not.

Teambuilding can't only be accomplished with feel-good exercises at staff retreats. It is something we forge by defining and reminding one another of the greater purposes we serve and acknowledging our interdependence is pursuing and reaching advancement goals. When we help each person understand the part they play in helping their organizations achieve significant, sustainable societal impacts, we bring out the best in those who seek to make a difference with their lives.

Teambuilding and other advancement goals can be facilitated by outside experts. Once again, inside experts should not feel that such efforts are at their expense or undermine their credibility. None of us, no matter how good we are, should be offended if our boss wants us to get more training, either by sending us to workshops or by bringing trainers onsite. After all, training is an investment in our potential, and none of us should feel as if we have met our full potential until we, as Hamlet says, "shuffle off our mortal coil." But, we do have a right to be offended if those providing the training don't seek to meet us at our level of proficiency and, like a good coach, help us continue to build on it. A good coach would not come in and talk to us as if you had never played the game. He or she would watch our level of proficiency and show us how we can stretch and strengthen our innate abilities and further hone our already well-developed skills. All consultants and trainers in all fields have observed the same phenomenon: the most talented professionals and the very best organizations are the most likely to seek outside expertise to become even better, while mediocre professions and weak organizations insist they are at the top of their game.

The subtext of the AU case study was strong leadership and confident professionals who believed in the superiority of team play. Contrast this to low-functioning cultures where fundraisers are expected to act as "lone wolves" working from lists of prospects, many of whom are recently wealth-screened but not deeply connected to the institution and working with generic fundraising materials. It should be abundantly obvious and inarguable which system and approach is most apt to produce the greatest results, year in and year out. Yet, those without the benefit of experience in reasonably high functioning cultures, or no experience at all (including new presidents, deans, even new vice presidents of advancement and, yes, even board members), tend to think fundraising is all about asking. They think the business is about hiring fundraisers, arming them a list of prospects, and sending them out on the road. As the AU case study shows, it about so much more than that and involves so much more than mere asking. Indeed, asking is most effective when it is a culmination of a larger, interactive, multi-dimensional, and progressive process.

The Right Pace: Patient Persistence

In this story, we see classical building blocks of fundraising success including:

- Ms. Lemieux had a long and relatively positive history with the institution, including a moderate degree of familiarity (having attended campus events) and rewarding interactions with some university officials.

- Her real giving potential remained latent because her deepest philanthropic motivations had not been discovered.

- That potential was unlocked with a spark of attraction (between what she cared about and what the dean thought important to do).

- The dialogue between the dean and donor unfolded in a deliberative, interactive, and iterative manner (which supports the natural decision-making process for responsible adults).

- The dialogue moved from conceptual (conversations with the dean off campus) to experiential (interactions on campus with the deans, department heads, faculty, and students).

- University officials did not rush to the ask but waited until Ms. Lemieux was more fully informed.

- The dean asked permission to put a proposal in front of her to make sure she did not feel rushed or ambushed, because they sensed that it might be more than she expected.

- Any concerns raised by the donor were resolved as they arose (e.g., deploying the planned giving director to help her understand her giving options).

- A partnership of shared purpose was formed.

- The donor was kept fully informed on the status of the project (including struggles and setbacks) and, most importantly, what the dean had learned at each step and what he was doing to continue to adjust and adapt.

- The donor felt eminently satisfied with the process and outcome.

- The first gift was only a glimmer of her greater philanthropic potential.

In short, AU created the conditions that allowed her philanthropy to unfold and blossom.

The pattern described by the case study is consistent with major gift success across a wide variety of institutions. The most common underlying factors that make donors receptive to meeting requests from fundraisers are listed below. They often include a combination of positive recent interactions underpinned by a deeper, long-term personal affinity for the organization's mission.

The more of them you can check off, the greater the likelihood a fundraiser will be able to secure an appointment. The most important in the "recent" column is having previewed an idea they find intriguing.

For every one that can't be checked, the probability of securing an appointment decreases. If affinity is all in the past and has not been reinforced by recent interactions, every effort should be made to engage before a fundraiser is deployed.

Fundraisers should be deployed when these favorable conditions have been created. Without them, donors will reject the efforts of even the most gifted fundraisers.

Therefore, it is a poor use of everyone's time, talent, and resources to ask fundraisers to pursue prospects without the right affinity markers.

And it is impossible to evaluate the effectiveness of fundraisers without organizations first evaluating themselves on how well they have done at creating the right fundraising conditions.

The Future of Fundraising

RECENT	PAST
Intrigued by the idea to be discussed	Org had significant impact on them or loved ones
Trust person coming and/or organization represented	Cause represented speaks to personal values
Enjoyed regular, recent engagement with organization	Regard for org continues, has deepened with time
Feel valued and respected by org	Belief in the org's conscientiousness and efficiency
Respect and value the organization	Larger family, social circle also engaged, supportive, and appreciative
Belief in the org's ability to make distinct lasting differences	Affected by traditions and rituals
Feel honestly and fairly dealt with in previous interactions	Believes society needs more of what org is providing
Org at or near the top of their philanthropic priorities	Has always felt at home, rewarded when attending events
No worries of being hustled, misled, pressured, or ambushed	Believes representatives are exemplary culture-carriers
Feel as if they are in a position to be helpful	

When we study the donor who has given $1 million or more, we see that he or she has:

- Given to that institution for the past 15 years (the average number of years of previous giving for gifts of $1 million or more).

- Is highly satisfied with how the institution has handled previous gifts.

- Has discussed and negotiated the gift, on average, for 18 to 24 months before he or she sat down with the president over dinner.

- Likes the gift concept the president suggested because it resonated with his or her deepest career interests and/or personal values.

- Has made more money in the past year than in previous years.

The Right Priorities

Though not explicitly stated in the case study, one could impute from the details presented that AU had the right fundraising priorities. They are:

1. Retain current donors
2. Nurture and reward donor loyalty
3. Deepen donor connection
4. Create a stronger alignment between current donor interest and emerging institutional priorities
5. Acquire new donors selectively along the lines of emerging institutional priorities (when you do, repeat the process)

Most institutions, except the very new, would be wise to allocate no less than 80% of their budget and effort on the first four priorities and no more than 20% on the last one.

For many years, this will prove to be a startling assertion because the emphasis in their advancement operations is the exact inverse. Yet, all the data and the longitudinal information we have at our disposal, including analyses from the most successful fundraising organizations, year over year,

The Future of Fundraising

demonstrate, quite convincingly, that attendance to the first four priorities will prove far more predictive, sustainable, and productive than the inverse.

The next chapters, therefore, will:

- Address how each of these priorities can be most effectively addressed, in terms of specific strategies and tactics.

- Demonstrate how organizations with the right outlook, the right approach to teamwork operating at the right pace – at a more fully optimized fundraising potential – can accelerate the realization of their institution's mission promise.

- Show how the seeds of donor attrition are sown by short-sighted solicitations.

- Demonstrate how an emphasis on acquiring fewer donors more interpersonally proves to be far more productive and sustainable than rapid, impersonal donor acquisition.

He might use numbers but they appear plucked out of thin air where's the case, the evidence, the logic.

JAMES M. LANGLEY

CHAPTER 6
RETAINING DONORS THROUGH IMPROVED ACQUISITION AND RESPONSIVENESS

All too often the subject of donor retention begins with the receipt of the gift and with the need to thank and recognize donors in ways that are meaningful to them. However, the better place to begin is asking where the seeds of donor attrition may have first been planted. All too often it is the way the donor was acquired. So, let us first address how donors are acquired, in the most lasting and most tenuous ways, so we can learn how to reinforce the positive and mitigate the negative.

Strong institutions initially "acquire" donors by fulfilling their mission promise and providing lifelong value to their students. They acquire:

- First-time young alumni donors who are highly appreciative of the rich, personalized, and new-world-opening education they receive.

- First-time parent donors who are thrilled with the way that the child is loving their learning experiences.

- First-time major gift donors who see a way to give through the institution to achieve some significant, sustainable societal impact.

- First-time corporate donors by producing graduates equipped with skills and personal traits that correspond to corporate hiring ideals and/or by producing knowledge, through research, that spawns streams of innovation.

- First-time "friends" through a host of good deeds including all of the aforementioned as well as considerate town-gown relations and contributing to the economic and cultural development of the communities that surround them.

Institutions, for instance, with low student-faculty ratios that can more afford personal attention, provide more intimate learning experiences in and out of the classroom, and foster a sense of belonging with rituals and shared cultural experiences generally have higher rates of alumni participation. Students who have more opportunities to get to know professors are more apt to keep in touch with those professors well after graduation and to turn out for alumni engagement programs featuring top professors. In this and other instances, we see that initial donor acquisition at the most high-performing institution does not usually begin in the advancement operation. It begins by providing significant and lasting value to its stakeholders, which causes many of them to be receptive to subsequent friend-raising, volunteer, or fundraising requests. Institutions that provide less value, as perceived by their stakeholders, therefore, have a harder time acquiring and retaining donors and generally acquire and retain them in select areas within the institution that are more distinct and distinguished.

Engendering personal appreciation, therefore, is the most important step in acquiring donors. The deeper that appreciation, the more likely the prospect is to be receptive to a fundraising request, especially if it resonates with what they valued most about the institution and/or with what they think is most important to accomplish with their life. Further engaging donors in the life of an institution is often the second level of acquisition for many in that it brings them closer to the institution which they already appreciate and allows them to see how it is not only relevant to making who they are but how it could be a partner in the fuller realization of who they want to be and what they want to do with their lives.

We need to realize that donors to learning institutions are not acquired by fundraising but by good deeds done, leaving their constituents with deep **appreciation**, and then by offering satisfying **affiliation** that builds on that appreciation by allowing them to see and experience the greater **agency** of that institution. Imagine how absurd it is, then, to task fundraisers to raise money without understanding the predicates of philanthropy and/or without an ongoing institutional commitment to further engendering appreciation, encouraging meaningful affiliation, and demonstrating future agency. Imagine how essentially the same fundraising techniques plied at two different institutions – one that consciously and assiduously creates the conditions that will allow them to continue to produce future donors and one that assumes fundraisers create prospects irrespective of what they do – will produce profoundly different results. Imagine how one institution, living off its reputation for once having created those conditions but much less committed to or effective at creating them today, puts fundraising in the position of siphoning off accrued goodwill, and with fewer and fewer prospects of doing so with every passing year. When institutions seek to harvest more this year than they plant for next year, they sow the seeds of their own decline. For too many, the drop in fundraising results in any given year will be the first indication of long-term, undetected decline.

This is why all institutions, including the most high-performing ones, need to understand, as soon as possible after the first gift has been made:

- Did the donor seek out the institution or give of their own volition without being prompted by any institutional fundraising effort? (For too long, we have assumed that people gave because they were asked, yet new knowledge, including one recent study conducted by Campbell Rinker, revealed that only 9% of new donors gave in response to fundraising material sent to them; in other words, they initiated the gift without prompting.)

- Did they give out of deep gratitude to one person or two, in remembrance of a good deed done to them at a critical moment, in deep appreciation of a particular education program or field or study, or out of a broader sense of pride in some larger institutional accomplishments?

Appreciation → Affiliation → Agency

- Did they give to retire a debt of gratitude or to invest in the future (or both, such as those who might give to ensure that students in the future would benefit from a particular experience as much as they did)?

When we know the "personal why" of someone's initial gift, we can then be far more proficient at stewarding that gift in a more personal way, whether or not they gave to an unrestricted fund or for a designated purpose, by playing back what each donor, or groups of donors, might find most rewarding, including:

- Informing donors who gave modest amounts for financial aid support - because they had friends in school who struggled financially or dropped out - how that fund has helped reduce the average debt load for current students.

- Letting donors who gave to the restoration of an iconic building – because it held so many good memories for them – that it has become the hottest hangout for current students.

- Sharing with a donor who gave to a memorial fund to a particular professor – because that professor had been so instrumental in his intellectual development – that 25 other donors had cited the same reason.

- Letting a donor who gave $10,000 to the student investment club – because she got her first job as a result of the experience in that club – know that the club's return has beaten the Dow Jones market average for the fourth straight year.

The Future of Fundraising

So, while the most significant acquisition of alumni donors, for instances, can be traced back to a person, program, or experience at their alma mater that added value to their lives, institutions can greatly increase their chances of retaining those donors over time and thereby magnify their potential for giving ever larger gifts and, ultimately estate gifts, by understanding and reinforcing the individual impetus of each gift.

Understanding how we actually acquired a donor, rather than simply assuming it was because they were asked, and trying to understand why donors gave, requires a very different skill than is usually associated with institutional advancement. It's called listening. It's so important and such a sea-change from the way business has and is being done at so many places, that we need to ask for a moment of silence to reflect on the fundamental importance of listening, really listening to our donors. Just as we once believed the key to sustained fundraising success was asking but now realize that most skilled fundraisers are the most curious listeners, we now realize that the key to donor retention is not about the material we send out but about the testimony that we cause to come in and how we respond to what we have learned.

The reason that we lose donors is that we don't hear what they are trying to tell us, including:

- They feel as if they have been asked too much.
- They think their giving isn't making much of a difference.

JAMES M. LANGLEY

- They don't find our case for additional support compelling.

- Their emotional connection to our institution has weakened (or grown stronger elsewhere).

- They think we should not spend so much on fundraising materials and/or administrative overhead.

If we heard these concerns when they first began to form, we could alter our communications and outreach accordingly, but that's still a big "if" at many institutions.

The reason that we fail to optimize the potential of many of the donors we retain is that we don't hear what they are trying to achieve with their lives, including:

- What issues or causes are most important to them.

- What their overall philanthropic priorities are and where our institution ranks.

- To which institution or nonprofit organization do they contribute most of their time, talent, and treasure.

- Which organization has done the best job of stewarding their gifts.

This lack of knowledge causes us to assume too much or be too complacent about donor preference and donor loyalty, thereby allowing less complacent organizations to develop stronger affinities with those we consider to be "our donors."

The Future of Fundraising

All of this can be mitigated, however, with more proactive listening exercises and by listening through all available means. Examples of proactive listening include:

- Surveys.
- One-on-one interviews with donors (which can be conducted by advancement staff, students, volunteers and others).
- Focus groups.
- Feasibility studies.
- Requesting constituent reviews of strategic plans or unfolding initiatives.
- Question-and-answer sessions at events.

While all of these are laudable and helpful in strengthening donor affinity, there is a tendency at many institutions to do these on occasion, rather than thinking of each and all as constants. The more constantly and comprehensively institutions listen, the more consistently they pick up on shifting attitudes, growing concern, or eroding confidence and the more quickly they are able to correct their course. For instance, an alumni survey run every five years, while useful, will never yield as much important and timely information as ongoing surveys with representative alumni. Spot surveys and polls can be conducted through call centers normally dedicated to one-way phonathon calls; by alumni relations staff before, during, and after events; by students conducting alumni discovery interviews, or by college and university officials when meeting with alumni groups, to name just a few.

High-functioning organizations believe that listening is a constant and seek to do so with all available means.

Those means might include:

- One-on-one meetings with donors and volunteers, and aggregating information for each not only for the purpose of a single donor profile but a cross-section of donors' opinions and attitudes.
- Q&A's during events and/or follow up interviews or surveys.
- Stewardship interviews.
- Listening through the annual fund call center.
- Spot polling through social media on a host of critical issues.
- Seeking feedback on pending major initiatives.
- Polling to understand the impact of a campus controversy or crisis.

Institutions that engage in constant listening demonstrate a high degree of accountability, non-defensive, and "porousness" by providing many ways, big and small, for intelligence about and from key constituents to continue to flow in.

The most astute institutions understand the power of forensic listening at key points in the donor experience. For instance, if donors are acquired through rapid, impersonal means, such as giving days or traditional phonathon calls, or if acquired in ways that don't reveal donor's deepest philanthropic motivations, it would be immensely wise to call, write, or otherwise contact as many new donors as possible and to ask:

- Could you tell us why you made this gift?
- What was the impetus for it?
    - Was it a fond memory?
    - Was it something that resonated with your personal values?
    - Was it given out of appreciation for something we have done or something that you hoped we would do?
- How does it correspond to what you consider to be your highest philanthropic priorities?

In just a few minutes, a lot can be learned about donor motivations, and once motivations are better understood, stewardship activities can be more effectively customized to reinforce donors' reasons for giving. And, in just a few minutes and with a few questions, your institution can leave these donors feeling much more valued and appreciated.

A year or so after a gift has been made, it would prove wonderfully helpful to ask donors:

- How can we be better stewards of your giving?
- How can we better demonstrate the impact of your giving?
- How does our stewardship compare to other organizations to which you have given?

- What has been your most satisfying giving experience and what can we learn from it?

- Is there anything you would you like us to aspire to that we have not?

In just a few minutes and with just a few questions, institutions can demonstrate how much they value the support they have received and just how intentional they want to be in keeping their donors satisfied. And in the process, they can learn about what is working, what isn't, and what could be done better, thereby allowing them to further customize their donor relations.

For those donors who become the most loyal, deeply involved, and contributory, it would be more than astute to ask:

- If we are to remain the organization that inspires your highest trust, what about us do you hope will never change? Why?

- What about us, in your estimation, needs to change most quickly? Why?

- When have you been most satisfied with your relationship with us? When were you the least satisfied with us?

- What could we do more or less of to demonstrate your value to this organization?

The gravitas and authenticity in such questions makes key donors feel increasingly like valued insiders, a phenomenon that is important in and of itself but also, when felt by donors, is highly predictive of future giving, including major estate giving. And these questions can be asked by anyone interacting with donors – from phonathon callers to major gift officers, and from alumni relations specialists to board members – at any time, not as part of a single survey or study.

Beyond reinforcing the personal why of giving, high-performing institutions steward giving by:

- Providing timely, personalized thank-you's after each gift, ideally from those who have most directly benefitted from the gift.

- Producing annual reports for their endowment givers.

- Noting and celebrating years of loyal giving, especially the hallmark anniversaries when someone gives for 5 years, 10 years, 15 years, and so on.

- Providing impact reports wherever and whenever possible.

Now let's contrast two different cultures. (See the diagram on the following page.)

The first, a *reflective* culture, understands it has and will continue to acquire adherents through the good deeds it has done and aspires to do and seeks to understand how its request for private support will find the greatest receptivity and resonance with them. The second, a *non-reflective* culture, believes it's the role of fundraising to raise more money each year and gives little thought to receptivity, resonance, or how its value proposition is perceived by its prospects.

REFLECTIVE CULTURE	NON-REFLECTIVE CULTURE
Seeks to discover what prospects find most valuable and hopeful	Seeks to acquire most donors through rapid, impersonal means
Creates fundraising appeals that tap into prospect receptivity and resonance	Seeks to reacquire them every year using the same means
Proposes partnerships of shared purpose	Proposes categories for giving that are determined by the institution
Listens to the "why" of giving	Thinks of stewardship as thanking and recognizing done by Advancement
Deepens affinity by responding to the "why"	Rarely understands why its donors gave their first gift
Offers purpose-driven engagement opportunities	Doesn't know where it ranks in its donors' philanthropic priorities
Seeks reinvestment based on previous and projected societal ROI	Doesn't notice or repair donor loss in its pursuit for more $$

As stark as the contrast between these two, and as sensible and sustainable as the reflective culture seems, most institutions have too many non-reflective characteristics. They persist with tried-and-increasingly-untrue telefund scripts, spray-and-pray direct mail techniques, mass e-mailing, gift officers cold-calling people they hope will be prospects, planned giving brochures mailed to alumni just because they're of a certain age. Obscene amounts of money are spent on call centers that find fewer and fewer prospects taking the calls, dismal open rates on e-mail and response rates on direct mail of 1% or less, gift officers who have to make 30-40 requests to secure one appointment, and planned giving officers peddling deferred giving instruments as if they were appealing and valuable in and of themselves.

The Future of Fundraising

The simple but all too ignored or avoided truths of non-reflective fundraising include:

- The more rapidly we acquire donors through impersonal means, the higher the attrition rate.

- The more we attempt to reacquire donors the following year using the same means, the less receptive they will be and the more likely we are to lose them for good.

- The greatest rate of attrition is after the first year of giving; it is particularly high with online donations.

- Most donors feel sufficiently <u>thanked but under-informed</u> about the impact of their giving, and most donors say they will give more money than in the previous year if their means increase and if they better understand the impact of their giving.

- The more we focus on one-year results, especially to balance our budgets, the more we sub-optimize the potential of our prospects and undercut our long-term fundraising potential.

- That the vast majority of institutions have suffered a slow but steady loss of donors in the past 20 years.

- The vast majority of gift officers struggle to secure appointments with the prospects in their portfolio; when they are successful, the vast majority cannot convert the first meeting into any further interaction with those prospects.

[margin note: SHOW ME THE DATA]

All too often these facts are met with a shrug and the explanation that such successes or lack thereof are "consistent with industry standards" or "national trends." Yet, those standards and trends are what they are because so many continue to engage in the same shortsighted, non-reflective practices. And we wonder why we're losing both donors and development officers. Yet, any movement toward the reflective characteristics will stem donor attrition and allow us to begin building stronger communities of shared purpose.

The place to begin building more sustainable fundraising practices is at the point of acquisition. Acquisition is the first impression we make on donors. If they are left feeling in any way rushed, misused, hyped, or squeezed, the second attempt will be rejected at a high rate. Even the most responsive stewardship will not compensate for the most unsatisfying first impressions. The following analysis, done by Louis Diez, Executive Director, Annual Giving, Muhlenberg College, demonstrates the power of careful, personal acquisition. He contrasts one organization that acquires only 1,000 donors a year but retains 90% vs. one that acquires 2,000 donors a year but retains 60%. Both organizations begin with 5,000 donors. At the end of seven years, the impersonal shop has the same number of donors despite its impressive acquisition rate. The one that acquires half as many, but in more personal ways, ends up with over 50% more donors.

THE FUTURE OF FUNDRAISING

	Retains	Acquires	Total number of donors	Retention rate
Year 0			5000	90%
Year 1	4500	1000	5500	
Year 2	4950	1000	5950	
Year 3	5355	1000	6355	
Year 4	5720	1000	6720	
Year 5	6048	1000	7048	
Year 6	6343	1000	7343	
Year 7	6609	1000	7609	

	Retains	Acquires	Total number of donors	Retention rate
Year 0			5000	60%
Year 1	3000	2000	5000	
Year 2	3000	2000	5000	
Year 3	3000	2000	5000	
Year 4	3000	2000	5000	
Year 5	3000	2000	5000	
Year 6	3000	2000	5000	
Year 7	3000	2000	5000	

[margin note: What is ind bnch mark?]

When Louis plugs in very conservative revenue projections into the same model (which he can provide), the results are dramatic. The rapid acquirer raises $663,650 in seven years; the careful acquirer raises $2,633,347 — more than four times in the same period.

# $10k donors (5%; 3+ years)	# $25 donors	**Total Raised**
	5000	**$125,000.00**
	5000	**$125,000.00**
54	4946	**$663,650.00**
54	4946	**$663,650.00**
54	4946	**$663,650.00**
54	4946	**$663,650.00**
54	4946	**$663,650.00**

# $10k donors (5%; 3+ years)	# $25 donors	Total Raised
	5500	$137,500.00
	5950	$148,750.00
182	6173	$1,976,818.75
200	6519	$2,167,725.63
217	6831	$2,339,541.81
232	7111	$2,494,176.38
245	7364	$2,633,347.49

As compelling as this data is for some practitioners, it is equally startling and unsettling for others. So many are so deeply acculturated to mass acquisition and to the repetition of mass acquisition techniques, that the thought of doing anything less than building as much gift volume as possible each and every year seems terrifying. If they slow down the volume of acquisition, they fear, dollar amounts will plummet, and heads will roll. Yet as the models above demonstrate, there is a more steady and certain path to sustained fundraising success if institutions stop seeing stewardship as the sole means of retention and start seeing more methodical, interpersonal acquisition as the way to set the stage for more personalized stewardship and, together, the keys to building stronger communities of shared purpose.

One of the most common concerns expressed about a more methodical approach to donor acquisition is one of cost. "That sounds all well and good," say some, "but isn't it more expensive?" In other words, "Won't it make the overhead rate for fundraising appear much higher and thereby cause the powers that be to frown on us?" Yet, as the modeling above shows, the methodical approach will yield significant higher dollar amounts over time, even when we plug in very conservative assumptions. The reason should be clear: fundraising is not, and never should be, thought of in one-year increments. Yet, if we objectively evaluate fundraising results in any given year, we will see that the most significant results have far less to do with what was done in that year and far more to do with the accumulative effects of previous years. For instance, the largest gifts, those that may comprise 80% or more of your "annual results," come from donors who have given for at least 15 previous years. The vast majority of estate gifts come from donors who have given at least 20 years.

> **RUN THESE NUMBERS FOR YOUR OWN SHOP**
>
> What percentage of your "annual results" come from donors who have given for at least 15 previous years?
>
> What percentage of estate gifts come from donors who have given for at least 20 years?

Even the dialogue between donors and organizational representatives around specific gift commitments usually spans more than 12 months. And, yes, what you claim to have raised in the name of giving days can be traced back to relationships and processes developed over several years. In addition, the most important work you do this year in the name of fundraising will not realize its greatest fruition for years to come. So, if you fixate about how much you can squeeze out of any given year, and tie your identity to that goal, you will squander all you have inherited from the past and fall well short of what you could achieve in the future.

The deep obsession with one-year results and the treating of fundraising as a series of distinct one-year increments have undermined long-term fundraising potential and caused many donors to fall away, having grown weary for the calls for more each and every year, with no more understanding of how more has created anything better or made a lasting difference. The question, then, is not if we can afford more methodical, personalized acquisition but whether we can afford not to do it.

We must be more honest about what is and is not working in the name of fundraising, and what will be less and less supportable in the years ahead – in board meetings, in the deliberations of presidents and their cabinets, and in the gatherings of advancement staffs, including at professional meetings. All parties need to gather around the facts and assess them without seeking blame or offering defensive explanations.

In the next chapter, we will show:

- The importance between striking the right balance in retaining loyal donors on the basis of loyalty and retaining more cause-oriented donors on the basis of annual impact.

- Why traditional events and engagement activities are proving to be less attractive to donors and how they can be engaged more meaningfully in the life and work of any institution.

- How to engage and involve donors with future-oriented initiatives.

- How advancement leaders can evaluate the effectiveness of their engagement strategies to determine which they need to stop, which they need to rework, and where fresh approaches are required.

- How to engage highly successful, immensely talented donors who have considerable time constraints.

- How to build a stronger culture of accountability that will allow institutions to instill deeper levels of confidence in their most discerning donors and thereby inspire higher levels of future investment.

CHAPTER 7
NURTURING AND DEEPENING DONOR RELATIONS

The more institutions move away from getting gifts in pursuit of annual totals and toward creating partnerships of shared purpose, the more they will learn to listen and align at the outset of their interactions with prospects. By doing so, they will be in a better position to respond in ways meaningful to their donors in that all-important first year, thereby strengthening the basis of the newly formed partnership. The more that is done, the more institutions can focus on nurturing and deepening donor relationships with every passing year.

Just as with fundraising, adaptive advancement cultures need to work the strategic intersection between declining philanthropic behaviors and increasing philanthropic behaviors when it comes to nurturing and retaining loyalty.

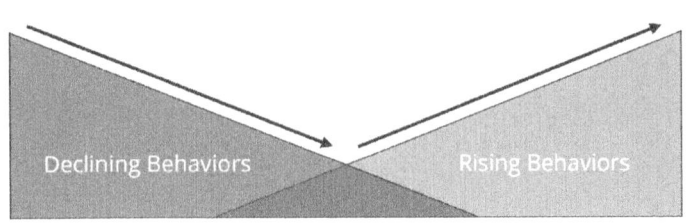

The Strategic Intersection

The Future of Fundraising

For those who have given loyally and quietly, so often those from the Silent and Baby Boomer generations, no recognition matters more than loyalty itself. A personal anecdote will illustrate this point. As a young executive, I took the advice of Penelope Burk, whose research showed the most loyal donors are not motivated by graduate giving societies, (e.g., silver, gold, platinum, or the equivalent) only by the acknowledgement of loyalty itself. At her recommendation, we sent letters to 1,000 of our most loyal donors, listing off their years of giving, and thanked them for their remarkable loyalty. Within days of receiving those letters, those donors began contacting us saying things like, "I didn't realize I missed 1984. My wife was very sick. Can I buy it back?" We were astonished by the fact that a little over 300 of those donors who had received that letter didn't realize that their loyal giving was not always in unbroken consecutive years. When they realized it was, they asked if they could give in the present to cover those missing years. Loyalty and the record thereof was that important to them. Of course, we made it possible to do just that and created the first, or among the first, "buy back" options for annual donors. In another position, a decade later, I did the same at another institution with almost exactly the same results.

Such a deep commitment to loyalty is touching to witness but much more likely to be seen in older generations. This is not to say that younger generations are less worthy or impressive, only that they act on their convictions in different ways. For instance, they may be very loyal to a cause, purpose, or community but not to a particular institution. This then is an example of how important it is to nurture loyalty as a virtue with older generations while finding more meaningful ways to recognize and reinforce the way it manifests in younger generations.

Ways in which loyalty can be recognized rewardingly for older generations include:

- An annual letter acknowledging each donor's record of giving.
- Admission to a loyalty society, often named for the most loyal donor, after a certain number of years, perhaps starting with five.
- Graduated benefits according to key anniversaries of giving, such as:
    - A customized, campus tour after five years of consecutive giving.
    - A group consultative session with the president after 10 years.
    - A free campus parking pass, gym membership, or theater membership after 15 years.
    - Being named a Presidential Advisor after 20 years .
    - Asked to review and opine on key planning documents, afforded front row seating, and recognition from the presiding officer at all major campus events after 25 years.
    - Named Distinguished College Citizen after 30 years with numerous rights afforded including serving as honorary marshals at

every convocation and commencement (please note the underlying strategy is to afford more "insidership" after each increment of five years of loyalty, not hand out tonier merchandise).

- Using quotes from loyal donors in various fundraising appeals.

- Featuring loyal donors in various publications.

Once again, let us not forget the importance of listening, no matter how long donors have given or how deeply they may be involved. Indeed, for those donors who become the most loyal, deeply involved, and contributory, it would be more than astute to ask:

- If we are to remain the organization that inspires your highest trust, what about us do you hope will never change? Why?

- What about us, in your estimation, needs to change most quickly? Why?

- When have you been most satisfied with your relationship with us? When were you the least satisfied with us?

- What could we do more or less of to demonstrate your value to this organization?

While meaningful to donors whose deepest affinity is with the institution itself, these approaches can be less moving or motivating to those animated by a particular discipline or attached to particular department. They will want more exposure to the pith of a particular program, including recent developments in knowledge creation, or its application to current and emerging challenges. Institutional affinity is a declining behavior while affinity with a particular discipline or program is a growing tendency. Institutions that fail to recognize these patterns continue to offer only broad institutional events (e.g., homecoming, reunion, parents' weekend, etc.) and may be overplaying to declining behaviors at the expense of fostering rising behaviors. In most instances where traditional institutional events are featured, and institutional affinity is assumed, we see decreasing attendance and participation from younger generations. Institutions that preserve some traditional events but augment them with faculty lectures, accomplished alumni presenting on the latest development in their fields, and alumni-to-alumni discussions on topics of shared concerns (e.g., raising autistic children, finding work-life balance, caring for aging parents, etc.) demonstrate the ability to work the strategic intersection.

Yet, one of the great failings of overplaying the traditional hand is the assumption that the choices, affinities, and loyalties developed as students will persist for a lifetime – that engineering majors will maintain an primary affinity with engineering or those who studied English will remain more interested in literature than in any topic. This assumption, when used to determine the allocation of prospects to various schools, colleges, and departments, hold "all engineering grads belong to the College of Engineering" or "all former English majors belong to the College of Arts and Letters." Some institutions assume a deeper affinity may lie with the activity or organization where students spent most of their extracurricular time – be it the school newspaper, field hockey, or some other club sport, Greek life, or student government. There are two major flaws with such thinking:

1. Most of us, whether at age 30, 40, 50, or 60, do not maintain a lifelong interest in what we found riveting at age 19, 20, or 21. In most instances, we develop new interests that overtake the older ones.

2. No one actually asked the prospects or donors what area of the institution they would deem most worthy of their time, talent, and treasure.

Indeed, this tendency to think of alumni and other donors as somehow frozen in time and just physically older versions of their student selves has created any number of barriers to engagement, giving, and re-giving. Therefore, the first steps toward improved retention must be to abandon those assumptions, to let donors decide which part of the institution is of greatest interest to them, and to realize that philanthropic spirit is and always will be far more animated by hope than by nostalgia and that donors will always give more of themselves to create a better future than to pay a debt to the past or alleviate a problem in the present.

With that understanding, we can focus our efforts on not just engaging donors but putting them on future-oriented tracks including:

- Increasing chances for student success
- Improving the persistence and graduation rates for specific student populations

- First-generation students
- Under-represented groups especially for local ascendant populations
- Facilitating transfers from community colleges
    - In recognition of new demographic realities
    - To respond to workforce demands
- Reducing barriers
    - Improving mental health
    - Developing successful study habits
    - Coping with adversity
- Preparing for the workplace
    - Career development
        - Where the jobs of the future will be
        - How to create your own destiny
    - Interview preparation
    - Making the most of the first three months on the job
- Developing new corridors of learning
    - Pedagogical innovations that seek to improve learning outcomes
    - The more effective use of learning technology in classrooms, libraries, and residence halls
    - New approaches to experiential learning

- Practitioner-professor team teaching
- Re-imagining cooperative education (traditionally alternative semesters of study with semesters of work)
- Adaptive internships (traditionally one student in one workplace for the summer)
- Team internships
- Class projects engaging civic, business, and non-profit leaders

- Increasingly important frontiers of knowledge
    - Research foci
        - Why
        - Potential applications
        - Opportunities to leverage grants, expand scope and impact
    - Collaborative, cross-disciplinary efforts
        - New models
        - New insights
        - New hopes
- Community Service
    - Strategy
        - Needs assessments vis-à-vis institutional strengths

- How it can better relate to mission advancement
  - How it could inform or be informed by classroom teaching
  - How it could inform or be informed by research

While these examples are far from exhaustive, they represent the kind of activities and pursuits that learning institutions are involved in every day. We don't need to make up activities to keep donors more involved. We simply need to plug them more frequently into what we do as a matter of course. To achieve that, institutions need:

- Leaders who understand the importance of more substantive engagement, adopt it as a strategic imperative, and emphasize its importance to internal stakeholders.

- The willingness of many engaged in such activities to become champions and interlocutors.

- A growing awareness that dialogue and interactive demonstrations will deepen donor affinity far more than one-way promotional pieces and second-hand explanations.

- A reordering of emphases and priorities, including a rethinking of traditional communications and events, to ensure more customized constituent engagement is viewed as a replacement, not an addition to, congested agendas.

The Future of Fundraising

The last point is of the utmost importance. Under the best of circumstances, it is difficult for people, and therefore institutions, to change even when the need to do so is pressingly palpable and enormously well-documented. Leaders of necessary, adaptive change must not layer new expectations on top of already onerous ones. They must be willing to review the current calendar of events, donor engagements, communication strategies, and other commitments to see how they comport with the need for necessary adaptions and improvements. They must develop criteria for reviewing the status quo and then determining which activities should be eliminated and which can be retrofitted or redesigned. Then, when they meet a degree of inevitable internal resistance, they can assert: "Surely, if we have found the time and resources to…

- "Produce expensive, glossy, generic publications for general use, we can use our found time and recovered resources to produce more customized, content-rich material for our key constituents."

- "Entertain offsite, offering galas or golf tournaments in hopes those attendees will develop some affinity for our cause, we can use the same time and resources to provide our supporters what money can't buy – the opportunity to engage in purposeful dialogue with some of our most impressive doers about what greater good we could achieve together."

- "Stage brain-implodingly dull, self-promoting advisory board meetings and other dog-and-pony shows, we can certainly find the time and resources to invite donors into the best, most aspirational, more hopeful parts of our everyday lives."

Please note the suggestion that the preponderance of what an institution offers external constituents should be offered first, and done best, for those who have already given. That means affording current donors:

- The most attractive board slots, volunteer options, and advisory opportunities.
- First pass at the most appealing onsite events.
- Meaty, emotion-inducing events designed just for them.
- The most carefully crafted, thoughtfully composed communications.
- The most inside knowledge and access.

As commonsensical as this precept may seem, the simple fact is that all too often too many institutions extend more red carpet treatment to prominent prospects they hope to attract than to loyal donors who, over the course of their lifetimes and in their estates, will provide the most significant return on any dollars invested in them. In some instances, the tendency to overlook the loyal partner we have in search of a lover we think we would like to have is noted and does deplete our standing in the minds of those who matter most.

As institutions seek to do away with events, activities, and communication that have proven less effective at building and sustaining communities of shared purpose, some will leave some external stakeholders unhappy – and some of those stakeholders may indeed express their displeasure. Yet, how, as new realities encroach, do we justify:

- Putting on pricey shows in tony venues when the fundraising return is so low and so indirect.

- Preserving traditional events when only a small fraction of constituents turns out for them.

- Recycling the same event attendees, many of whom seem more in search of a social life than in creating a better society.

- Expending precious resources on materials that are rarely read or, if read, rarely acted on.

- Covering the costs with precious unrestricted dollars that come from our most precious human resources – students, parents, and donors?

Advancement leaders help institutional leaders make those decisions by:

- Evaluating the allocation of resources across the panoply of advancement-oriented activities to determine which have attracted the most valuable constituents and caused them to commit more of themselves as a result.

- Presenting their bosses with candid assessments of which of those activities are the most and least efficacious – and which least and best justify the use of the president's time.

- Expressing their willingness to make difficult decisions when empowered by their boss to do so.

- Demonstrating how new approaches can be scaled and how large numbers of donors can be put on customized information tracks, while reserving engagement tracks for most loyal and most generous donors, and by showing how levels of engagement can be graduated accordingly.

- Showing how every vehicle previously used solely for fundraising can be converted into a two-way, dialogic vehicle (e.g., how phonathon banks can be used to conduct donor polls, interview first-time donors, and personalize other outreach activities, etc.).

True customization of constituent engagement also means providing donors with the level of engagement they want – not what institutions assume they want. We know, for instance, that institutions benefit the most from deeply engaging volunteers in:

- The contribution of exceptional talent (including high-level skills and wisdom born of considerable experience in demanding fields) for which most institutions could not afford to pay.

- The power of their example in attracting other skilled volunteers and inspiring younger colleagues.

- The fact that their financial contributions equal twice as much each year and ten times more in their lifetimes than passive contributors (if they were philanthropic before taking on a volunteer role).

- The powerful third-party endorsement that their deep affiliation represents, which gives confidence to other donors and constituents, both current and prospective.

For these and other reasons, institutional leaders seek to plug their most impressive volunteers into the most consequential roles or engage them as actively and deeply as possible. However, many donors do not want to give that much time or be that central to institutional decision-making. They are content in more observational capacities – be they intellectual, cultural, or athletic – or in participating in activities that are more purely enjoyable and less pivotal to institutional strategy such as institution-sponsored travel, traditional alumni gatherings, or seasonal festivities.

Some extraordinarily busy donors with much to offer may avoid joining standing bodies or making ongoing voluntary commitments, but efforts should still be made to make the most of their expertise in strategic ways. Many highly skilled donors could be thought of as potential pro bono consultants who could make invaluable contributions of even an hour's time, certainly if they gave a half day, and especially if they made themselves available for a full day. Many of them may have expertise in areas that learning institutions seek "outside help" for, including brand management, market research, cost containment, crisis management, strategic planning, team-building, investing, master plan development, and many others – for which too many institutions are too quick to pay those with less to offer. Indeed, many institutional leaders are pleasantly surprised by how many exceptional, talented alumni, parents, and friends feel complimented when asked to lend their expertise and are more than willing to do so under the right circumstances and with sufficient advanced notice. In fact, many of them wish institutional leaders sought them out more often for the acumen and insight, and less for underwriting their pet projects. Here is one cautionary anecdote:

> A very wealthy man invites two peers and me out for a round of golf at one of the nation's most prestigious golf clubs. When the foursome reaches the fourth tee, the generous host lets it be known that "my president is coming to see me this Thursday." It was, he thought, a subtle reference but one that might impress his chums given the fact he is an alumnus of a world-class university and had arrived at such station in life that he was being sought after by its leader or, as he said, "my president." His chums immediately picked up on the indirect boast and sought to counter that bit of preening by submarining his assumptions.
>
> "Gee," said one, his voice dripping with dry, flat sarcasm, "I wonder what he wants."
>
> The implication of his jibe was clear. "Your president is coming to see you for one reason and one reason only – he wants your money, and that's all you mean to him."
>
> The second piled on a few more scoops of sarcasm, this time expressed with faux wonder. "Don't tell me, don't tell me," he said, "He's bringing plans for a new building!"

> So, the second was saying, "Not only is he coming to see for your money, he's going to ask you for what he wants and what you could care less about."

Every president should have been so fortunate to witness the same, not only to play golf with three fine gents on a storied golf course but to have been afforded an unvarnished view of how donors think of, and prepare themselves for, requests for presidential visits. Key takeaways from this anecdote include:

- Many donors see right through requests for the president to meet with them.

- While some hope otherwise, many assume it will be not only to solicit a gift but for a project that they have had little input on and which does not map with their animating passions.

- Donors are not complimented to learn that the institution is, once again, seeking their support, but they are deeply complimented if they feel a president is genuinely reaching out to them for their expertise, especially if it is on a highly critical matter.

- Too many institutions live up to donors' suspicions; too few surprise them by seeking their engagement in a weighty topic.

The keys to engaging considerable but time-constrained donors include:

- Identifying areas, places, and moments where their expertise will prove most valuable and consequential.

- Determining the person with whom they could consult to achieve the greatest effect; many donors would rather consult directly with the authority who has sufficient skill and experience to discuss issues peer-to-peer, to grasp the importance of the expertise offered, and to implement the most germane recommendations.

- Finding a time that is most convenient to the donor, which could include evenings and/or weekends.

- Looking for ways to make the consultation as enjoyable and rewarding as possible for the donor, including ways to interact with the potential implementers or beneficiaries of the advice, and allowing the donor to come alongside them as they are doing their work.

- Avoiding putting on a show for donors, humoring them, and treating them differently simply because they are wealthy.

- Letting them know what was learned, how their advice was applied, and what happened as a result.

- Debriefing the donors to see how the consultation unfolded from their perspective, if there was good chemistry with the recipients of the advice, and if they found it sufficiently worthwhile to be receptive to doing more (when all works well, productive and amicable relations between donor consultant and the institutional recipients continue to unfold and set the stage for voluntary financial contributions).

The Future of Fundraising

Whether it is with a purpose-driven donor who wants to see their investments through to impact, the donor who seeks to be enjoyably immersed but not put to work, or the hyper-busy mogul willing to give occasionally of their expertise, the secret is to listen and to seek the best possible alignment between their passions and propensities and the institution's strategic needs. In so doing, we should remember and seek to obviate the most common complaint of the highly skilled volunteer: "They ask too much of my time and use too little of my talent." And, while we know that donors who invest the most time and talent into an institution are far more likely to give most generously according to their means — while passive observers, especially those who rely on institutions to help them fill up their social calendar, are most likely not to give more — we cannot be in the business of making donors do what we want. We can only provide them with a rich, interesting menu of real opportunities to advance an important purpose, and let the donors decide.

That said, the descendant and ascendant donor relations trends are becoming clear. More and more want, expect, or hope:

- To be engaged with kindred spirits and those who share their convictions, rather than by constituent group (e.g., alumni, parent, legacy donor).

- Personal expression of thanks from the recipients of their funds rather than receiving generic thank-you's from people they don't know or figureheads.

- Institutions to not just thank them but better inform them as to the impact of their investments.

- Not to be recognized just as a level of giving or placed in a giving society and certainly not asked to give again to move up into an artificial category.

- Institutions not to waste money on gifts or merchandise to recognize their giving, often countering such efforts by saying, "You should use that money to advance your mission."

- To be treated like outcome-oriented investors rather than like nostalgic or sentimental institutional boosters.

- To be kept informed by the recipients of their giving or the implementers of their investments rather than receive general reports about the health of the institution.

- To learn more about institutional accountability, efficiency, and other information that will reassure them that their investments will retain, if not gain in value over time.

Donors who stand to make the most significant investments want something far more substantial than vision statements, elevator pitches, or wish lists wrapped in pontifications posing as strategic plans. They want to review plans presented by leaders with the foresight to anticipate societal need, the courage to differentiate and the determination to deliver value. When they see evidence of that kind of leadership, and the results that stem from it, they will consider their investments well-stewarded and will be far more likely to give again.

The Future of Fundraising

Yet, even rare leaders, possessed of the most remarkable attributes, must be intentional about building cultures of accountability, fully aware of how hard it is to achieve and sustain and how easily it can begin to slip. Creating cultures of accountability, particularly as it relates to fundraising, entails "golden rule" thinking — not just asking what we want from donors but what they want from us, and doing all we can to find that happy, sustainable medium.

WHAT ORGS WANT FOR THEMSELVES	WHAT DONORS WANT FROM ORGS
A culture of philanthropy	A culture of accountability
Major gifts	Major impact
Endowments (to make their future more secure)	Adjustments to constant change
Loyal following	Promise keeping
Impressive facilities	Adaptive structures that facilitate human performance
Reputation	Relevance
To be held in awe	To be heard
Unquestioning trust	Proof of trustworthiness
Event attendance	Substantive engagement
Captive audiences for speeches	Participative problem solving
Giving as a precondition for engagement	Engagement as a precondition for giving

Builders of accountability will understand the importance of making it an institution-wide ethic, not just the job of a few people with "stewardship" or "donor relations" responsibilities. They call others to that ethic and put some teeth in their expectations by:

- Requiring everyone who interacts with donors to file contact reports, especially noting anything that is revealing of donor satisfaction or provides more insight into donor propensity (in this way everyone contributes to and benefits from collective field intelligence).

- Compiling and comparing contact reports regularly to look for favorable or unfavorable trends in donor perceptions; equipping all field representatives with questions for all to ask as a form of ongoing market research.

- Polling of donors to understand what triggered a donor's original gift, what keeps them giving, and/or what caused some to lapse.

- Conducting, through all these means, a more comprehensive feasibility study for any pending fundraising initiatives.

Special attention should always be afforded to institutions' most loyal donors. One way of developing an ethic of appreciation for such remarkable people is to learn their names. In high-functioning cultures, the names of at least the 25 most loyal donors, as measured by years of giving irrespective of amount, are known by many, including members of the governing board, presidents and their cabinets, academic and athletic leaders and just about everyone in advancement. When this is achieved, many people will be provided with authentic, spontaneous affirmation of their importance when such donors attend events or somehow cross the paths of institutional representatives. It means so much to so many donors to realize that they are known and appreciated by people who make institutions work, not just the people who raise money.

Indeed, spontaneous, unstructured stewardship may have a far greater impact on donors' various pro forma responses, just as an unexpected expression of love and appreciation from one's spouse or partner is received as particularly pleasing and romantic. Asking senior officers, board members, and others in your organizations to carry thank you cards with them so they can send spontaneous, handwritten notes when they see the impact of philanthropy, such as:

> "I heard a concert last night in the hall named for you. I hope you know how much joy you bring to so many so regularly."
>
> "The speakers coming to campus as a result of the lecture series you endowed are bringing out record numbers of students and deeply enriching their campus experience."
>
> "I have taught several students that you have supported with scholarships. They would not be here otherwise, and we would be the lesser for it."

Donors want to hear how their gifts continue to make a difference. It doesn't matter if they know the writers of these notes, in fact, it can mean more when they do not. Such unexpected affirmations, as with all of us, will make their day and help your organization demonstrate that it believes that stewardship is everyone's business.

As more institutions pursue, and in some cases secure, eye-popping gifts from the powerful 1% at the top of the giving pyramid, they need to make sure that they are not so obsessed with principle gifts and major gifts that they leave modest donors feeling dwarfed or relatively inconsequential. If they do, they may conclude they can have a greater impact elsewhere. Institutions must be attentive to potentially losing donors who are more purpose-driven, who simply want to be something more than one of thousands in annual totals, or a bit more red mercury in some campaign-counting thermometer. It is all too easy to forget that these very same donors, if retained over time, become the most likely sources of future major gifts and/or the largest estate gifts. We can raise major gifts and retain modest donors and purpose-driven donors if we design more campaigns around the societal return to be generated by giving through our institutions and less around the dollar totals we'd like given to us.

Conclusion

In recent years, more and more institutional leaders and advancement leaders have come to understand the importance of stewardship and donor relations in building and sustaining private support. Those fields, too, have grown in prominence and in their ability to identify and share best practices. As a result, many more donors are better served and many institutions are being rewarded with stronger donor affinity and, therefore, the potential for continued if not greater future support. However, there are very few organizations that elevate those functions to their highest strategic level. While it is immensely important to thank, recognize, and engage donors in the life of the institutions they support, it is also more and more essential for donor relations and donor retention to be recognized for what they really are – two of the most important benchmarks of institutional performance and viability. As such, that information must be brought to the top of organizations and analyzed in detail to make sure they understand the long-, mid-, and short-term reason for donor loss, what its early indicators are, and what might be the most effective corrective actions.

To achieve those important ends, more institutional leaders will have to elevate the function, and more donor relations professionals with more strategic mindset and better market research skills will be required.

Here are several significant steps that institutional leaders can take in this direction:

- Ask their advancement leaders, or consultants supporting them, to develop a plan describing how donor relations can be practiced at the most sophisticated and strategic level.

- Create a job description for the person to lead it that will attract high-quality candidates either from within or without.

- Empower that office to act as the philanthropic conscience of your culture.

This would entail defining donor relations as the means by which an organization seeks to establish a more perfect top-to-bottom institutional accountability in donor relations and to monitor, coordinate, remediate, and optimize any function or area influencing donor relations, including:

- Monitoring gift agreements on a regular basis to ensure institutional obligations are being met.
- Reviewing contact reports with donors to build more insightful donor profiles.
- Relaying information on changes to donor profiles or donor preferences to relevant institutional representatives.
- Serving as an ombudsperson for donor concerns or requests.
- Monitoring the overall rate of donor attrition as well as according to key variables – years of giving, level of giving, level of involvement, etc.
- Producing "State of Donor Relations" reports.

A high functioning stewardship office should be encouraged to remind everyone, from the president down, how donor relations – individual or collective – can be better managed. When Peter Drucker observed astutely that "culture kills strategy," he was warning us how the worst of a culture can undermine even the best of strategy. By the same logic, however, it must be true that the more conscientious a culture becomes, the more it inspires and enlivens the most effective and far-reaching advancement strategies.

The Future of Fundraising

In the next chapter we will:

- Examine the best ways to not only acquire new donors in light of new philanthropic realities but to do so in a way that increases the likelihood of their retention over many years.

- Explore the disparities between what institutions want from donors and what donors want from institutions, and how we can begin closing those gaps.

- Explain what is most and least effective in acquiring donors, making sure we don't confuse correlation for causation.

- Differentiate fundraising practices that appear to work, showing how in fact they work only for a short time and often at the loss of greater philanthropic potential.

- Call out practices that no longer work.

- Share best practices for acquiring new alumni donors, new individual donors, new parent donors, new foundation support, and new corporate support.

- Reveal the common denominators of successful donor acquisition across the board.

James M. Langley

CHAPTER 8
ACQUIRING NEW DONORS

Many scanning the table of contents for this book might have been surprised to see this topic – donor acquisition – not addressed until the eighth chapter. It is, after all, what many think of when they think of fundraising – acquiring donors at the point of solicitation, whether it be for annual giving-level or major gift donors. That assumption leads to the belief that most of the work done by most fundraisers involves setting up meetings with prospects to ask for their support. Assuming that philanthropy is inspired and harvested in a single meeting is akin to assuming that wine comes from a bottle, jelly from a jar, or pumpkin from a can. Yes, you can access nature's fruits in those ways, but there's a whole lot more to the story about how they got there – and what it will take to produce more.

In earlier chapters, we have established that philanthropy, the fruit that all fundraising seeks to harvest, begins in the fertile hearts and minds of those who are so grateful for their good fortune – even though it may pale in comparison to those with vast fortunes – that they must share it with others but do so in a way that comports with the lessons their lives have taught them. In other instances, it is born of the souls of those who have suffered or seen loved ones do so, and who then resolve, quite remarkably, not to descend into self-pity and victimhood, but to do all they can to keep others from being similarly afflicted. They are the kind of philanthropists who conclude:

"We can't live life over again, but we can give others…"

- A safer, warmer, more constructive childhood than the one we experienced.
- A better education than the one we enjoyed.
- A comforting, ennobling spiritual life that we were too late in discovering.
- The opportunity to pursue dreams that the practicalities of our lives prevented.
- A way to alleviate emotional struggles that haunted our lives or those of our loved ones.
- The chance to begin building better careers than our lives afforded us.
- The hope of reducing or eliminating the incidence of diseases that afflicted us or our families.

The roots of true philanthropy are deeply personal, and that is why it is so important for learning institutions to go in search of them and do all they can to nurture them – by giving hope and validating the hopes that such people invest in them. They can do this by:

- Listening more closely for the stories that brought such remarkable people to their doors.
- Respecting the lessons that their lives taught them.

- Realizing those lessons were often learned from the most searing experiences and should not be toyed with or exploited.

- Showing them how they turn the barriers their lives have put in front of them into gateways for others.

- Demonstrating how they can give through your institution to bring about measurable and immeasurable improvements in the lives of others.

- Nourishing their hopes with stories of differences made.

- Allowing them to see your mission in action.

Please note, then, the most important steps in acquiring new donors are:

1. Identifying those with philanthropic intent, either on the basis of previous giving, civic engagement or other evidence of a desire to improve society, rather than chasing wealth or casting fundraising nets more broadly through mass mailings or other broad appeals.

2. Capturing the attention of those prospects in such a way as to cause them to see the potential of your institution to bring about the changes that have been long important to them; this includes projecting purpose with real conviction and gravitas; frothy acquisition techniques are far more likely to draw less serious donors who will turn over more quickly and turn off more substantive ones.

The Future of Fundraising

Engagement can occur at four levels, as detailed below. Each complements the other and many prospects who become donors progress from one to the other. However, too many institutions have relied too long on Informational and Consumable engagement.

Prospect Engagement Levels

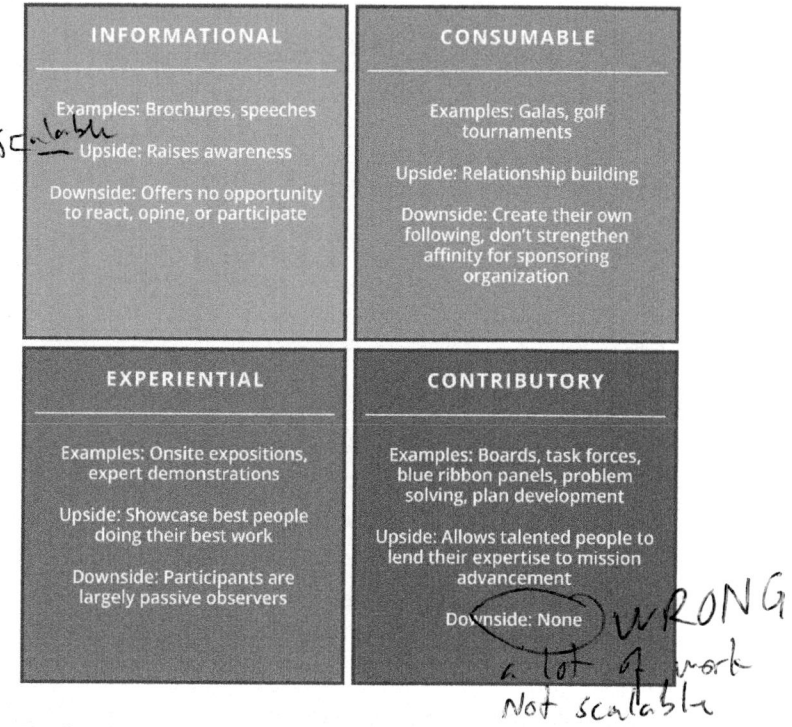

INFORMATIONAL	CONSUMABLE
Examples: Brochures, speeches	Examples: Galas, golf tournaments
Upside: Raises awareness	Upside: Relationship building
Downside: Offers no opportunity to react, opine, or participate	Downside: Create their own following, don't strengthen affinity for sponsoring organization

EXPERIENTIAL	CONTRIBUTORY
Examples: Onsite expositions, expert demonstrations	Examples: Boards, task forces, blue ribbon panels, problem solving, plan development
Upside: Showcase best people doing their best work	Upside: Allows talented people to lend their expertise to mission advancement
Downside: Participants are largely passive observers	Downside: None

Fundraising is a process that we can make deep or shallow, and everything in between, but we know where those with the deepest purpose-driven roots will generate the most philanthropic fruit – if we will but take the time to think beyond now or this year's haul.

HOPING DONORS GIVE	GIVING DONORS HOPE
Give generously to us!	We seek to meet a greater social need or opportunity
We need more support to cover our rising costs	Here's how we plan to make an even greater impact
Do you see how impressive we are?	Together, we can make a greater difference
Our goal is to raise megabucks	Here are carefully crafted budgets for 3-5 outcome-oriented initiatives
We're looking for more big donors	Our loyal donors are living endowments and the wellsprings of most major and estate gifts
Give us the opportunity to make a killer pitch	Join us in exploratory conversations so we may define shared purposes and goals
Thank you for giving	Here's how your giving has had a significant and sustainable impact

The best way to see the superiority of the "deep field," hope-giving approach is to observe and measure the differences between fundraising practices that work once, or just occasionally with some donors, to those that prove less damaging and more productive over time again and again and with most donors. The trouble with so much of fundraising and a reason why we are losing donors with every passing year is this terrible tendency to study, repeat, and emulate what worked once without realizing each repetition further depletes donor interest and discourages the philanthropic spirit. The following examples will help make this point:

- A young practitioner attends an annual giving presentation at a fundraising conference and "learns" from a well-intended presenter that the key to fundraising success is "asking six times." Indeed, this impressive presenter has data to show a spike in positive responses after the sixth ask. The young practitioner does not realize that the presenter has unwittingly confused causation with correlation by failing to note that the spike in affirmative responses came at the end of the calendar year, when the vast majority of loyal donors make their annual commitments. And, of course, the presenter has only measured what happened once. We know, however, that over-asking is the single greatest reason for donor attrition.

- A new president observes his Advancement VP repeatedly nudge a prospect during a solicitation, causing that prospect to increase the amount first pledged by 25%. On the drive back to campus, the VP says, "Always take the first amount offered as an opening bid. If you keep pressing, they'll give more." The president takes the advice to heart and resolves to incorporate the technique when he is soliciting gifts without the VP. The president never asks the VP if that prospect ever completed his pledge or gave again. Nor does he learn, until it's too late, that most of the school's best prospects were avoiding his VP like the bubonic plague, either having been nudged one too many times or having heard from their peers about his presumptuous treatment.

- After reaping a record harvest on their giving day, a college concludes that the keys to success were the catch phrase "Golden Rule Day" – a play on the song lyrics "School days, school days, good old golden rule days…" and the fact that their athletics team's primary color is gold, that the student cheering section is called the Gold Den, and their favorite sign to wave says, "The Gold Den Rules!" That quadruple entendre won the day, he thought. He did not deconstruct the numbers to see how many gifts were made by loyal donors, some of which came in at lower amounts than in previous years, or note the fact that 27% was raised by two young volunteers who tapped into the high regard in which they were held by their peers and who were saying privately to themselves that they were not inclined to do the same because of alma mater's controlling, bureaucratic oversight. The clever words had only the most remote correlation to that day's success, but the author of them will repeat them again and again.

- A dean, at the advice of the Advancement VP, takes a donor to lunch and solicits a $5.2 million gift for promising translational research on macular degeneration. The donor readily, even enthuseiastically, agrees. The dean returns to campus, walking on sunshine and regales the faculty and anyone who will listen about her captivating pitch including some of her most well-chosen, convincingly articulated words that made the donor's pupils dilate in wondrous awe. She does not know that the VP has secured that commitment previously from the donor but wanted the dean to conduct the solicitation as a sign of respect to the donor. She fails to mention that the donor had been giving to support macular degeneration research to various institutions for 21 years and that the disease was prevalent in his family history. The dean's boasting influences others to follow her example. They spend too much time trying to wow their prospects and are much too quick to solicit causing that institution to lose the support of viable prospects whose generous support could have been developed over time and in a more respectful way.

- An independent school head announces to his board that Exupery Academy will exceed its ambitious campaign goal seventeen months ahead of schedule. The bar chart he uses to show year-by-year results has the more meager results of his predecessor in blue bars and his much higher totals in crimson, hoping that subtle suggestion as to the difference he has made will not be lost on his bosses. He does not note, nor does most of his board realize, that the largest gifts received during his record years were one or two very large estate gifts, the vast majority of whom had given for decades before they died, had enjoyed amicable relationships with several school heads, including his predecessor, and were second or third generation alumni of the school whose children and grandchildren had also attended. As a result, the school head, having convinced himself of his fundraising prowess, assumes all he has to do is ask but as he works his way through prospects with the deepest connections, he notices fewer and fewer prospects agreeing to his solicitations, and more and more refusing to take an appointment with him.

- A planned giving director is over the moon after a sweet old couple agreed to a $2.3 million charitable remainder unit trust (CRUT), particularly because she had been touting CRUTs for some time in direct mail pieces sent to all alumni over the age of 60, in the Legacy Society newsletter, at the annual luncheon for legacy giving, and in private meetings with various planned giving prospects on the planned giving web page, which she had long argued needed to be featured more prominently. She did not realize the couple was not motivated by the CRUT but by a shared determination to leave a healthy portion of their estate for a purpose they had believed in most of their married life – scholarships for students most exemplary of community service. The couple thought it was "cute" how the planned giving director kept emphasizing what the trust would pay them in their lifetime, because they didn't need the money and were planning on using the payout for current gifts to their favorite kind of students. Nonetheless, the planned giving director leverages the gift of the sweet old couple and convinces her boss to double the budget for direct mail featuring CRUTs.

These anecdotes reveal several realities of fundraising that must be better understood if we as a culture are to improve our ability to nurture and sustain the philanthropic spirit that makes its possible. They include:

- It is all too easy to declare a particular fundraising approach "worked" and to produce some results as proof. However, when an organization has grown an orchard from good deeds done, especially over generations, it produces philanthropic fruit that can be harvested in any number of ways, including some relatively shortsighted and inept ones. Donors give not because of those fundraising practices but despite them, in the same way donors give to political candidates not because their campaign hounds them night and day with e-mail requests but because those candidates espouse values that resonate with their own. Imagine, then, when such "proven practices" are adopted in larger form. This is why so much mythology and substandard methods accrue to fundraising practice. When the orchard is full, anybody can shake a tree – with their right hand or left hand, or hit it with a spade, or drive a truck to it – and thereby take credit for dislodging the fruit and having it fall into their basket. But if their methods are too rough some fruit may fall prematurely, and many trees may be damaged in the process. For the field of fundraising to more fully mature, more practitioners imagining themselves as the fundraising equivalent of Little Jack Horner who "sat in a corner eating his Christmas pie"(philanthropy) who then "put in his thumb, pulled out a plum, and said, "What a good boy am I!"

- Seeming short-term fundraising success is an outgrowth of a much longer process – including the formation of donors' values, the ability of an institution to repeatedly and constantly deliver on its mission promise and to do so in such a way that it has a profound personal impact on no end of constituents, which then makes those impressed and grateful souls receptive to an outreach from said institution, which is only the first step in a longer exploratory process of alignment seeking, which, if reached at a conceptual level turns into an iterative negotiation in pursuit of a compact of shared purpose, all of which often obviates the need for a typical solicitation.

- Some practices that seem to work once or twice prove damaging to building more lasting and productive relationships with donors. Yes, we can squeeze one end of a tube and demonstrate that our exertion had something to do with the desired product, say toothpaste coming out the other end. But the fundraising tube, like the gift pyramid, is not self-populating. Donors don't crowd in there hoping for a good squeeze then say, "Well if was good for you, it was good for me." And it isn't a closed tube. Hard, inconsiderate, self-serving squeezes can repel donors out the other end and sometimes far away, never to return.

So, let's stop saying these practices "work" and are therefore worthy of repetition and emulation:

- Emails with miniscule open rates (leading legions of others to conclude your institution is the world's largest producer of impersonal boringness).

- Direct mail with a 1% response rate (and a 99% turn-off rate).

- Giving days when little or no attempt is made to engage or more deeply engage those who gave.

- Catch phrases (clever words are no substitute for conscientious intention and diligent execution).

- Phonathon scripts and associated annual giving techniques repeated even as alumni participation has declined over 30 years.

- Raising money through annual giving to balance the institution's budget which is of such low philanthropic appeal that it places fundraisers in pursuit of the least likely dollars with the highest rate of expenditure of their time and talents at the expense of the most likely dollars, and which causes emerging donors to see the institution limping from year to year and therefore less worthy of large, long-term investments.

- Urging people to give the equivalent of one Starbucks coffee per any increment of time (philanthropy is the fuel of social improvement, not a spit cup).

- Cold calls on prospects that only occasionally connect with the chronically lonely (while causing others to wonder why you have been reduced to such desperate measures).

- Deploying fundraisers armed with brochures presenting bucket categories of giving.

- High-gloss, low-content collateral fundraising materials.

- Lecturing prospects on the need to give, give back, or give generously (the generous don't need the lecture and the non-generous will remain unmoved).

- Idealizing alumni as a gaggle of pom-pom waving boosters rather than critical thinking constituents.

- Projecting institutional attitudes that are condescending, paternalistic, patronizing, or self-aggrandizing toward their prospects or infantilizing of them.

- Fundraising metrics that in no way acknowledge or build on anything emphasized in this book or ever written by an intelligent practitioner.

Unfortunately, this list could go on. The way to move beyond it is to look much more objectively and from a multi-year perspective at what really works, then reducing or eliminating practices that work once for some and never work for many others, ever. But let's be clear, it's not the vehicle – be it telephone, direct mail, brochures, or others; it's when these vehicles are used to push out messages but not listen, to blanket rather than target, and to extract support by promising little or nothing in return to society or those they serve.

These are the reasons why most institutions suffer the greatest rate of donor attrition among first-time donors – and why most never get them back.

- Acquiring them in rapid, impersonal, aggressive ways.
- Urging them to support institutional need.
- Failing to discover their deepest giving motivators.
- Re-soliciting them in the same way they were acquired.
- Repeatedly re-soliciting them.

The more we automate acquisition, the more we must personalize retention, and do so at the earliest opportunity. The more we personalize by learning what is most personal in each prospect's philanthropic journey, the more donors we retain. The more patient, personalized tortoise beats the get-it-now hare. Further, the hare is likely to have lost most of its donors for good, largely because of poor acquisition and a lack of timely, personalized follow-up. In other words, not only does the hare lose more financial support, year over year, but

The Future of Fundraising

the hare has less and less of a chance of catching up to the tortoise with every passing year. The tortoise maintains and increases market share in a declining market, and the hare gets more and pinched by encroaching realities. Unfortunately, institutional fundraising is and has been dominated by hares and hare-centric leaders, including presidents and boards, who are too obsessed with one-year results, looking only at the fruit yield after each harvest, not the health of the trees or the sustainability of the orchard that produces them.

To drive the point further home, imagine a group of new leaders arriving on the scene at places suffering from high attrition rates who then resolve to improve their donor retention rates by focusing solely on improved stewardship practices and better donor relations. Those leaders, and the additional emphasis they place on retention and the more resources they allocate to it, *will* lead to higher rates of retention but they will never be as successful as those leaders who reduce, mitigate or eliminate weak donor acquisition practices. Simply put, improving donor acquisition – by being more deliberate about aligning institutional capabilities with donor's convictions – is the key to improving donor retention, which, in turn, is the single most productive pathway to more sustainable fundraising success. No institution will get close to the 10% attrition rate without such an approach, not without more personalized interventions after the first gift and well before the second solicitation.

More sensitive, substantive, and sophisticated donor acquisition will also require institutions to recognize and, in many cases, repair damage done by putting the fundraising cart ahead of the relationship horse, or, in many instances, pushing a horseless cart at every occasion, at every constituent who crosses their threshold.

Acquiring Alumni Donors

For many alumni and other donors and, more poignantly, lost donors or donors who give to other organizations but not to their alma maters, too much of higher education employs the "Venus flytrap" model of fundraising. The institution works on presenting an alluring image and bidding donors to draw closer, while its fundraising jaws are ready to strike when they do.

For alumni, the proposition being put forward too often looks like this:

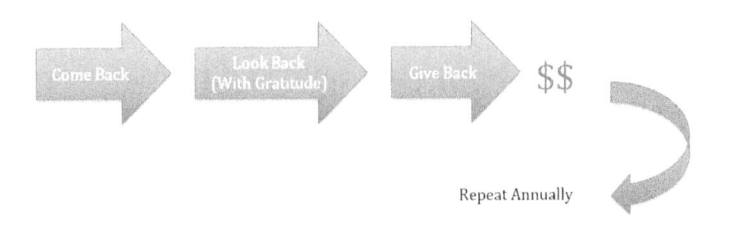

Come Back → Look Back (With Gratitude) → Give Back → $$ → Repeat Annually

Such a deal, eh? Is it any wonder that alumni, according to path-breaking research conducted by Witt Consulting say one of their major reasons for *not* giving is, "My alma mater does little to reach out to me besides asking for money"? Is it any

The Future of Fundraising

wonder that the volume of annual alumni giving has declined for a quarter-century? They sense that the end goal of every engagement proposed is "more money." Indeed, at too many institutions, that is exactly what advancement operations are expected to achieve as their primary goal.

Please note the false and eroding assumptions that underpin the model depicted above. They are that alumni:

- Are nostalgic about their time on-campus (i.e., they have a deep and abiding emotional connection to the place).

- Still have an interest in traditional alumni gatherings such as homecoming and reunion.

- Want to have a dedicated space (i.e., an Alumni House, even if it isn't on campus).

- Should be grateful for their education, no matter how much it cost, how much debt they accrued, or how a good of a job they have been able to secure.

- Will be receptive to repeated calls to "give back" in gratitude for purposes we stress, including the ever-sexy "unrestricted income" or "president's discretion."

- Having given once, will become addicted to the process and want to do so again and again whenever the request is issued.

- Will give loyally their entire lives and when they reach their 60s or 70s will be on the lookout for literature

> from us as to how they can leave most or all of their estate to us.

Yes, these assumptions are stated in such a way to demonstrate that, if pushed too far, become absurd on their face. Yet those assumptions, with varying degrees of institutional presumption, persist in many places and cause increasing numbers of alumni to stay away because "it's always about needing more money."

Yes, there are alumni who are so deeply grateful and loyal in their giving that it would suggest some of those assumptions are true to some degree but the vast majority of those donors are of "the Greatest Generation" and "Baby Boomers." We see the culmination of their loyalty in magnificent gifts given late in life and generous estate gifts announced after their passing. But time claims more of them every year and younger generations are not following in their footsteps. Contrary to the beliefs of some, particularly those who drink heavy quaffs of the elixir, Wishful Thinking, these younger generations are not going to reverse lifelong patterns of not giving and staying away and decide in the 40s, 50s, 60s, and beyond that they suddenly want to behave like loyal Boomers once did. If we know anything about philanthropic behaviors, indeed human behaviors, it is that once they are formed, for good or for ill, that it is highly unlikely that they will change or only change as the result of a powerful disruptive force. Institutional leaders or advancement professionals who think they will counter these trends through force of personality or clever marketing are sadly mistaken.

We can see these same assumptions in the plans of a campaign that employs the following process.

Institutional Aspirations → Funding Categories → Campaign Goals → $$

"Institutional Aspirations" are usually the result of a "strategic planning process," which is not truly strategic because it is yielded from internal deliberations, not external needs assessments. Even though these aspirations may be tested later with a feasibility study, they are not the product of true strategy - the means by which internal aspirations are shaped by external realities.

"Funding Categories," traditionally considered institutional building blocks, are usually characterized as:

1. Endowment (preferably unrestricted)
2. Capital Improvements
3. Student Support
4. Programmatic Support

These categories are then dressed up as much as possible and presented in impressive campaign collateral material. But remember, this approach is based on the following assumptions that the consumers of these materials are appreciative, if not affiliated, alumni enthusiasts who will remain receptive to, if not resonant with, calls to respond to institutional needs. Those are dated if not dangerous assumptions. Consider:

- In recent years, there have been no more than 15 unrestricted gifts of $1 million or more given in any year to all of American higher education, which is comprised of more than 4,000 separate institutions.

- Giving to capital improvements in recent years represents, on average, more than 15% of the total given.

- A U.S. Trust Study of high net worth philanthropists revealed little interest in these categories and to traditional campaigns themselves. According to the study, **"The great majority (76.8%) reported donating to neither capital nor endowment campaigns. Only 11.1% of high net-worth individuals indicated they contributed only to a capital campaign, and 8.7% indicated they donated to both a capital and endowment campaign."** Of the small percentage who did give for this coveted purpose, it is safe to assume that many were long-term loyalists, including long-serving board members who were 60 or older.

This approach, that of asking donors to give to the aforementioned categories, is increasingly out of sync with current and emerging philanthropic realities because:

- More alumni have student loan debt, and the more indebted they are to a lending agency the less indebted they feel to their alma mater, hence the 30-year decline in annual alumni giving.

The Future of Fundraising

- Fewer and fewer alumni remain affiliated with their alma maters, especially in the traditional ways (alumni clubs or chapters, alumni specific events such as homecoming or reunion, or engaging in purely nostalgic activities).

- Alumni are no longer the largest source of support for American higher education. (Foundations are.) [wow]

- Alumni who do give want more choice and say in their giving.

- Alumni are far more likely to give to achieve something in the future than to give back in gratitude.

So, a long-established way of thinking about how to make a case for institutional support, one that was heavily reliant on large amounts of alumni fealty, needs to be tossed. The fact that it persists is symptomatic of a larger problem – a growing gulf between what institutions expect from their alumni and what their philanthropic alumni expect of them. Factors contributing to this gap include:

- The failure of many presidents to place a value on listening to alumni, acknowledging their concerns and frustrations, identifying areas where alignments of interests can be formed, and creating greater awareness among internal stakeholders on the essentiality of achieving such alignments.

- Accounting for gifts in such a way to make it appear that alumni and other individuals actually chose or designated their gifts for categorical purposes rather than the more specific intentions that guided them.

- Looking at alumni giving in the aggregate rather than by decade of graduation which allows them to remain blind to their dependence on Boomers and to the increasingly thinning numbers of giving alumni.

- Ignoring the fact that many young alumni do start giving after graduation but fall away in five years or less because the experience is so unrewarding and/or other organizations offer them more rewarding options and experiences.

Acquiring Individual Donors

If alumni have proven to be less and less receptive to giving to traditional categories, imagine how non-aligned individuals feel when presented with bland giving menus. In fact, that is why such menus or cases for support do not work. Non-aligned individuals are not looking around to ask which institution they should support but which institution has the best ability to advance the purposes they deem most important. Such individuals, particularly those of high net worth, behave like foundations – they are not just in the business of giving for its own sake; they have established giving guidelines and pre-determined which causes and purposes they give to, under which circumstances, and what accountabilities they will be seeking in return. They will, therefore, ignore or rebuff calls from fundraisers carrying the traditional portfolio of institutional needs, invitations to traditional events, and even open-ended requests for meetings with presidents. They will respond to those institutions that do enough homework to put forward an idea that triggers their specific philanthropic receptors.

To demonstrate this point, let's use a real case study, one with which this writer is intimately familiar.

Case Study

A senior advancement official, Jaime, accepts a vice-chancellorship at a prominent public university in Southern California. He and his wife buy a small but strategically located parcel of property three blocks away from the Pacific Ocean. Then the real estate market hits bottom during a recession. The recession lifts and the property, on paper, accrues value with every passing year usually at double-digit rates. After eight years, the owners are now, on paper, millionaires. That fact does not escape the notice of the advancement official's alma mater, which has recently acquired wealth-screening capabilities. Nothing that the advancement official has achieved in his career has attracted the notice of his alma mater, but this rapidly escalating piece of property has.

One day, Jaime answers his cell phone to hear a boomingly cheerful voice on the other end.

"Jaime! This is Dave!"

Jaime knows a number of Dave's, but can't place a name with this voice.

"Dave?"

Dave then lets it be known that he's calling on behalf of Jaime's alma mater, then invokes the name of its athletic mascot, "Go Capybaras!"

Jaime likes some sports, especially basketball, but it was not central to his university experience or to his personal identity. Further, he could never understand why the capybara had become the school's mascot, even as the largest rodent in the world. He had seen a few capybaras in zoos around the world, but they looked to him like large, hairy noses on four legs and were invariably lolling about in ersatz semi-aquatic environments. For those and other deep personal reasons, he found the invocation of mascot rather annoying.

"What can I do for you, Dave?" he asks with a slight menacing tone, as if to suggest, "But don't get carried away."

"I'd like to come see you," says Dave, as if it were an irresistible offer.

"When?" Jaime asks, hoping he will be doing something at the time requested.

"Anytime," Dave counters unexpectedly.

"Anytime?" Jaime asks with irritated incredulity.

"I'm in the neighborhood," says Dave.

This makes Jaime wonder if his alma mater, located 2,400 miles away, is making good use of its resources by dropping over-amplified agents employing forced affability to schmooze and ambush long-neglected but recently property-rich alumni. Of course, by now, Jaime realizes that Dave does not know that Jaime is a seasoned advancement official himself who can see Dave coming and is not impressed by Dave's approach. Yet, out of morbid curiosity and in search of material to be used at future training seminars, he asks:

"What do you want to talk about?"

"All the good things happening at the University!" exclaims Dave.

"I think I have some sense of that," says Jaime, "from all the brochures I've received in the last few months."

"There's a lot more I could share with you!"

Jaime has been contemplating a meeting with Dave just to see how awful the experience might be or to see how Dave would respond when he learned Jaime was in the same field, but Dave has already exceeded Jaime's tolerance for exclamations made in any given day, much less in a given hour.

"I'm sorry," Jaime says, "I have a big job and a lot of demand on my time."

Dave tries to get Jaime to reconsider by offering all sorts of options, including drinks after work, dinner, breakfast, or even a walk on the beach together. Jaime, thinking he'd rather press thumbtacks in his forehead, rejects every option.

Dave, upon returning to the home office, files a contact report saying Jaime had failed to qualify as a prospect. In fact, Jaime was very philanthropic, having given to several causes for more than 30 years. His student experience was uneven, but he remembered certain professors with high regard and appreciated the fact that he had been able to get a very good education at an affordable cost, so much so that he graduated with no debt and soon found good work. Under the right circumstances, Jaime would have given to his alma mater, but Dave never got close.

Dave's "cold call" approach was all wrong. Had Dave done a modicum of homework, he would have seen that Jaime had enjoyed a remarkable rise in his career, had come to be known widely for several innovations, and was often recruited to speak at professional conferences. If Dave had explored the possibility of Dave doing a pro bono seminar for his alma mater, perhaps sharing some of his innovative approaches, Jaime would have been happy to do so. If his alma mater wanted to adopt one of his approaches, Jaime would have been open to providing support for the pilot phase. Jaime, like many accomplished professionals, was not only interested in sharing his expertise, he felt an obligation to do so – and would, when asked, if the timing could be worked out.

Had Dave dug a bit deeper, he would have seen that Jaime served in the Army before going to school on the G.I. Bill. This would have been a good catch, because serving in the armed forces can be life-shaping (as it was in Jaime's case) and, therefore, influencing his philanthropic interests. Had Jaime learned from Dave that his alma mater was attracting a large contingent of vets, many of whom were struggling with PTSD, Jaime would have asked if there was any way he could have helped. Rather than cold calling Jaime and proposing to discuss "all the good things happening at the University," Dave would have been wise to have sent Jaime a report on veteran affairs and then requested a meeting to discuss that document. Jaime would have agreed to the appointment. Dave would have been even wiser had he asked the head of Veteran Affairs to reach out to Jaime with a draft of the report asking for feedback before it was made final. In that way, Jaime would have felt more complimented to offer his advice on a topic that he cared about deeply and to do so in a way that would be helpful to younger generations of vets. An even better approach would have been to send an invitation from the head of Veteran Affairs asking to meet with Jaime or for Jaime to return to campus to meet him and some younger veterans to review their plans and, as part of a select alumni committee on veteran affairs, draft a set of recommendations as to how that office could better serve its young veterans. Had his alma mater taken that more substantive approach and engaged Jaime in that way, that initiative would have been his highest philanthropic priority – and at a time when he had greater means than ever before.

This case study, then, yields a template for donor acquisition and hierarchy of options that looks like this:

1. Identify a prospect's deepest convictions or animating passions.

2. Recruit prospect to help create or shape a new initiative that resonates with those convictions or, if that is not possible, to:

3. Review and opine on an early-stage plan or, if that is not possible, to:

4. Review and refine a plan before it is made final or, if that is not possible, to:

5. Review a plan before taking a meeting with the initiative champion or, if that is not possible:

6. Review a plan before taking a meeting with a development officer.

7. Review a plan before being asked to give through some impersonal means, including direct mail, telephone solicitation, etc.

Our best model today for tomorrow's fundraiser is a foundations relations officer. Why? More and more individual donors (79% of all giving) are behaving like foundations, in that they:

- Have giving guidelines.
- Only consider proposals falling within their values vector.
- Expect organizations to do their homework, become vexed by, and screen out those that don't.
- Seek an alignment of purpose more than a social relationship.
- Want direct access to the project leader.
- Expect a budget for the amount requested.
- Want to see the means of evaluating a proposed project's progress.

- Give smaller gifts initially to test efficacy.
- Expect honest feedback on what worked, what didn't, and why.

Therefore, the fundraising skills that will prove more and less critical are enumerated below:

LESS CRITICAL	MORE CRITICAL
Social confidence	Content mastery
Gregariousness	Genuineness
Cold calling	Customized acquisition
Instinctive	Research oriented
Center stage engager	Off stage orchestrator
Tribal cheerleader	Impact broker
Unafraid to ask ASAP	Careful to time the ask
Masters elevator pitches	Seeks resonance with donors
Moves manager	Partnership developer
Closing skills	Negotiation skills

The first step is proving to be an increasingly important step in acquiring new donors. When it is achieved, or at least a plausible theory about a donor's convictions can be framed through various research methods, the probability of that prospect meeting with some institutional representative goes way up, and the potential for far greater fundraising efficiency is enhanced. If this is not achieved, the institution is much more likely to be ignored or rebuffed by the prospect – and to have the door closed on all subsequent requests. Further, the more prospects can be engaged at steps 2 or 3, the higher the probability they will invest their time and talent which greatly increases the probability of giving proportionately of their treasure.

From this evidence, we can then deduce four precepts for improved individual donor acquisition:

1. **Elicit much more than you solicit**. Interview your donors to discover what they most want to accomplish with their lives, then discuss where, when, and how your organization could actualize their most altruistic ambitions.

2. **Show more, tell less.** Stop telling, touting, and bragging about what your institution has done and start showing donors what it is doing in all its gritty glory. Their eyes will always be far more persuasive than your words.

3. **Make better use of volunteer talent; time and treasure will follow.** It's no compliment to be wanted for your money, but it's a huge compliment to be sought for your unique talent and to be trusted with a tough assignment that will allow you to apply it.

4. **Document how donors can give *through*, not just give *to*, your organization.** Donors are not interested in keeping your organization in existence if it is not getting better at delivering on its mission promise, so flip the script and start the dialogue with the greater societal impact your organization could achieve with their targeted investments.

The Future of Fundraising

Acquiring Parents

Parents, when compared with other prospect and donor segments, are the most apt to give shortly after becoming affiliated with an institution, to give the largest gifts within the first two years of affiliation, and to give to achieve short-term material gains – or, in other words, to give to those initiatives that bring about material improvements that will be realized while their children are still in school.

Parents become affiliated when their children are admitted (as do some grandparents). The giving is driven by gratitude stemming from having their child admitted and optimism about what can be achieved while their child is enrolled. The child, then, is the key interlocutor in determining the parent's outlook. The more gleeful the student is upon admission, the more delighted the parent. The more content the student becomes and the more they begin to thrive, the more grateful the parent. And the more students share with their parents about less-than-ideal material circumstances, the more apt the parent is to step in and say, "How much would it cost to …" Indeed, that is the recent trend – that parents contribute to functions, such as physical improvements in residence halls or support for specific athletic activities, and to improve an array of student services – from mental health counseling to study abroad.

The best time to acquire parent donors is in the first year of their child's enrollment, when all the aforementioned emotions are at their peak. At the end of the child's second year, parent giving declines – perhaps because the child appears well on their way to graduation and success, thereafter, leaving parents feeling as if there is little more they could or should do.

Yet, too many institutions place most of their acquisition hopes on a Parents Fund. While such funds allow parents to simply check that box and say, "I support all the schools my children attended," they do not optimize the parent potentials because:

- They lower giving ambitions by giving levels they suggest.
- They do not give parents choice or enough choice as to how the giving is designated.
- They don't create the means for active listening to, or active engagement of, parents.

Therefore, any process that does the inverse is likely to be more successful. Parent acquisition could be improved by:

- Surveying representative samples of parents in the first few months of the child's admission to determine their perception of what is working well and what needs to be improved – either from their perspective or that of their child's – then reporting on what the institutions have learned to all parents, what it plans to do in response and where private support will be most helpful.

- Conducting intimate conversations between high net worth parents, either on campus around major events or in the home towns as a part of a tour, with the vice president for student affairs, dean of students, or others who will be seen as being able to act on the advice received.

- Engaging parents around "portals of purpose" initiatives that correspond with their convictions and/or those of their children.

Indeed, the last option is the one most likely to develop the parent as a long-term donor because it taps into their deepest personal philanthropic interests, whereas the other options treat parents as only parents and thereby limit their giving potential with every passing year.

Acquiring Foundation Support

True programmatic distinction is the key to acquiring new foundation support because foundations are created to fund specific purposes. Funds are allocated by them after reviewing proposals submitted by outside claimants that project how they intend to advance those purposes, if funded. While there are still some foundations that will help build institutional capacity, such as funding new buildings, the vast majority give to programmatic initiatives that correspond with their stated values and purposes. Acquiring new foundation support, therefore, begins with the identification of internal thought leaders whose teaching, research and/or service foci map with a foundation's programmatic guidelines. Once again, we should avoid thinking of foundations as the means of getting a grant here or there but as potential partners of shared purpose. When we think in terms of pursuing partnerships, we think more carefully about the consequences of short-term miscues, such as:

- Failing to do adequate homework on the foundation's history, purposes, key officials, submittal processes, and funding guidelines.

- Rushing proposal development and missing obvious flaws or otherwise failing to fully manage the power of first impressions.

- Making ill-considered or unsubstantiated claims about the singularity of the proposed initiative, either in terms of focus or quality, without researching to see if others are in the same space and potentially doing better work – especially if those other institutions are or have been funded by the foundation in question.

- Not specifying how the initiative is to be monitored and evaluated and how the foundation in question will be kept abreast of those findings.

- Not projecting outcomes or desired results.

- Overstating budgets or failing to disclose other sources of support for the same initiative (which could actually make the proposed initiative more attractive because of the potential for collaboration between and among the funding parties, and the opportunity to leverage one another).

- Not being fully prepared to meet the actual or implied promises in the grant.

- Not being ready to steward the grant, including not briefing the grantees on their personal responsibilities to be accountable and steward the grant, and the very positive or very negative impact they could have on the institution's credibility – with the foundation in question and the others it is apt to share its experiences with.

- Failing to empower the foundation office to coordinate all grant submittals to prevent the appearance of internal competition, being inconsiderate of the foundation's expectations that proposals have been vetted, cleared and have the full backing of the institution in question, and having no enforcement of policies governing proposal submission.

Building lasting relationships with foundations begins with due diligence, respect for the other, taking the time necessary to build faith and trust, and being true to one's promises – as with all relationships.

Acquiring Corporate Support

Corporations give to realize corporate objectives, including direct objectives, such as strengthening its workforce, and indirect objectives, such as building a stronger brand by being a force for good in the community, which also enhances their ability to attract and retain a high quality workforce. Acquiring their support entails understanding and being clear-eyed about what they hope to achieve through their giving. The major reasons corporations have given to colleges and universities is to:

1. Identify and recruit rising talent with the most relevant skills.
2. Glean knowledge or content that gives them a competitive edge.
3. Build brand identity and consumer habits.

The first is the major and most prevalent reason. Strategic acquisition, therefore, requires an institution to analyze a company's workforce needs, both current and emerging, and to ascertain where it can be most responsive to them. Indeed, there is no better way to broker a connection with a company or corporation than to engage the appropriate official on that topic. This is further proof that current and emerging fundraising realities underscore the essentiality of listening as the first step toward partnership building. Assessing a company's workforce aspirations and then coming back with a plan as to how they can be met, while being honest about quantity and quality, creates the opportunity to be forthright about what your institution will need to produce what they want. This "strong posture," when assumed with companies and corporations, causes the funding request to be seen as an attractive business proposition and, therefore, worth a quick decision. Indeed, when done well, significant corporate support can be secured in less time than significant individual support, but it should be remembered that business partners will be quite adamant about the need of institutions to keep up their part of the bargain.

The Future of Fundraising

The second corporate interest, gleaning relevant knowledge, applies particularly to institutions with strong research programs, although there is plenty of room to think creatively about how any information gathered by an institution could be a value to outside entities. For instance, information gathered about student preferences for course options within a larger curriculum, might be an early indicator of the careers they are most attracted to, or data gleaned about student food choices or dietary options might be of great interest to those in the food business. Indeed, professors and researchers could work with business and industry to explore the potential intersection of interests, including research collaborations including shared space, translational research, clinical trials, and the development of intellectual property.

Again, the brokering of knowledge requires exploring which frontiers of new knowledge a company is most interested in, the relevance of your institution's research to it, and a determination if there is the potential for building a bridge between the institution's propensities and capabilities and the needs of the company. For instance, an institution may boast of research in an area of medicine that directly relates to a company's niche, but the research being done is at the basic science level, whereas the company is giving to funding research at the translational level. Candor and frank assessments at the outset about compatibility of interests, practices, and culture are critical. When those parameters are established, differences can be negotiated, and agreements can be forged in ways that allows each party to see the potential upside and risks going forward. As will be the case with so much "fundraising" in the future, building these kinds of corporate connections will require "content champions" to be actively involved in the negotiations and personally committed to stewarding the support received.

The third reason for corporate giving, to build brand identity or develop consumer behaviors, may be an implicit element in the other two reasons or explicit in the case of companies that explore the potential of more favorable product placements on campus or exclusive vending relationships. Such arrangements are usually contractual, not philanthropic, yet those two aspects of corporate relations must be closely coordinated in the name of overall partnership management. Company and corporate representatives often stress the need for "one-stop shopping" in brokering deals with learning institutions and modern realities dictate the need to do everything possible to facilitate giving and strengthen donor relations.

These new realities also point to the need for learning institutions to think about "total resource development" of which fundraising is a part. Not only can the receipt of one gift, let's say from a corporation, be viewed as a favorable leveraging opportunity for an individual donor or foundation interested in the same purpose, but more and more outcome-oriented initiatives will be more readily advanced if institutions adopt more of a "total resource development" model. For instance, most institutions pin most of their ambitions in the name of "student success" on traditional approaches and traditional giving vehicles, particularly the need for scholarships or financial aid for first-generation students.

The Future of Fundraising

However, imagine if more institutions showed companies and corporations a comprehensive plan that encouraged:

- Grants to incoming students who, if they met certain performance standards, would be eligible for.
- Co-op or internship opportunities, with graduated responsibilities for those who rise to the challenge.
- Incentive scholarships to high achievers in the third or fourth year of their studies.
- Intensive internships for high achievers nearing graduation.
- Or any combination thereof.

In this way, learning institutions could create stronger nexus between what they want – financial aid and internships – and what companies and corporations want – over-arching strategies in which they can target for their purposes and "contribute" that which makes best sense for them. This kind of model allows a variety of companies and corporations to participate in a variety of ways, all of which enhance the potential for student success. Further, learning institutions must acknowledge that there are lots of ways of getting money into students' hands – and the more options there are – the greater the likelihood of academic success, low debt loads upon graduation, and more rapid upward economic mobility for their graduates. Asking only for financial aid or scholarships says, in effect, "The only way you can help them financially is by giving to us." It would be far wiser and much more utile to say, "One of the ways you can help them is to give us scholarship support, but you could also help improve their chances of success by providing them internships and/or giving them jobs relevant to their majors."

Further, so many interesting, productive possibilities could unfold around rethinking co-op opportunities, internships, and part-time jobs for students. Getting students more internships – which enhance the potential for student success, and student appreciation that will convert to alumni affiliation – requires institutions to entertain more internship options that go well beyond the usual "one student in one workplace for one fixed period of time" to teams of students working on a project of strong interests to a particular company to one student being empowered to customize all wage-earning options to their specific interests.

All of this will require institutions to play a more facilitative role and to surrender some control in the name of building broader coalitions of shared purpose, fostering more creative thinking around how opportunities can be better customized to accommodate student and employer interests, and creating more dynamic models and modalities around the different kinds of student success and alumni job satisfaction. Indeed, one reason many colleges and universities have reassigned their career planning and placement functions to the advancement operation is to create a more strategic model of corporate relations that would allow the totality of corporate interests, especially workforce interests, to be managed as a part of a customized whole. Another reason is to take better advantage of alumni networks tied to alumni career interests. Once again, these trends are indications of efforts to adapt to new realities, to think about advancement as a more strategic, crosscutting function at the institutional level, and to break down "specialist silos" within advancement to facilitate those processes.

Yet, even this kind of thinking conceptually constrains the roles that companies and corporations could play in working with learning institutions toward greater community or societal ends. They limit the company or corporation to traditional roles supporting certain institutional purposes so that universities can support corporate purposes such as identifying rising talent, gleaning relevant research findings, and strengthening brand. However, if we return to the "purpose-driven model" of advancement, we see the potential for a host of other opportunities including companies and corporations being attracted to any number of "portals of purposes" and playing any number of roles in advancing those purposes. So much energy can be released and so much creativity can be directed at more strategic pursuits if we remember that the mindsets and organizing principles formed of necessity and utility in one generation can easily become the boxes and limiting factors of the next. Adopting the purpose-driven model and driving toward shared ambitions will allow institutions to more readily see the artificial and artifactual elements of their current organization and culture, as well as in their larger set of assumptions about how learning institutions relate to external entities and external interests and to streamline processes as more strategic pursuits unfold.

Part of this transition also requires adapting to a far wider range of corporate personalities, as manifest both in corporate leaders and corporate cultures, from the very conservative to the very radical. Corporate relations offices and jobs therein, therefore, need to be staffed with curious chameleons or curious ambassadors capable of researching very different types of companies and very different types of leaders, then developing plausible theories as to where their interests might mesh with those of the institution, deciding who is best equipped to begin brokering or advancing that relationship, testing and theory of alignment, negotiating differences, and crystalizing a compact of shared purposes that delineates the roles and responsibilities of each party.

Some, at this stage may be wondering if these suggestions seem to be assigning companies a larger role than their level of financial support warrants – which is about 15% of the total given to American higher education. But that's the traditional way of thinking about advancement – to allocate effort to the potential for raising dollars. In the new model, a new logic imposed by new realities unfolds like this:

- Institutions will see their fundraising abilities decline if they continue to ask for support for broad institutional purposes (e.g., student support, faculty support, capital improvements, and endowment).

- To raise and sustain levels of private funding, they must demonstrate the return on investment, most especially on the investment in tuition, which can be done in two ways – constraining operational costs and improving outcomes.

- Projecting ROI in terms of reputational gains will prove increasingly less satisfying to students, parents, alumni, and corporations. They will ask for more concrete measures and projections of student and alumni success.

- Achieving greater measures of student success that will be valued by all parties who share an interest in them will require closer collaboration between students and those who might employ them as students and as alumni.

Therefore, the ROI an institution makes in corporate relations should not be measured on the amount of money given in any particular year or series of years but:

- In the short-term, by the number of potential employers participating in the plan, the number of gifts, grants, and work opportunities in any form that are created and by relating the totality of those efforts to greater student persistence and higher employer satisfaction.

- In the mid-term, by the rate of job placement consistent with students' majors (including graduate school).

- In the long-term, by how all the parties involved feel about the efficacy and efficiency of the system created in terms of its ability to meet their needs and interests.

Demonstrating this kind of ROI over time will yield many other benefits including:

- Improved student recruitment potential, driven largely by positive-word-of-mouth generated by parents, alumni, and employers.

- Improved parent relations, stemming from the effort to enrich their child's education, to strike the right balance between the theoretical and the practical, and to convert the investment they made in a more satisfying life for their child.

- Improved alumni participation by allowing alumni to contribute their time and talent to achieve outcomes they find personally satisfying or professionally rewarding.

- Improved alumni relations in the form of former students for which the institution was responsible, for creating a system that served them well over time.

- Improved employer relations, for obvious reasons.

This new way of defining ROI provides a vivid demonstration of the limitations of the old fundraising and advancement models related annual expenditures to annual fundraising receipts and the far greater potential for purpose-driven model to create a broader coalition of shared purposes and to produce lasting results that are more satisfying to all.

Common Denominators of Effective Donor Acquisition

No matter the type of donor an institution is trying to acquire – individual, foundation, or corporate – fundraising in the future, if it is to be successful and sustainable, will require:

- Acknowledging that no donor is acquired solely by a fundraiser but that fundraisers can play an important role in facilitating first-time giving if certain prospects:
    - Have benefitted personally from the good deeds of the institutions or were directly affected by those who have.
    - Affiliated with it in such a way as to feel more personally fulfilled than was the case before affiliating and/or have witnessed good deeds done first-hand.
    - See in the institution, or some part of it, the capability to advance purposes they deem most worthy and vital.

- Accepting that it is an utter waste of time and resources — and a nuisance to prospects — and depleting for fundraisers when fundraisers are assigned prospects who have none of the aforementioned characteristics and/or when the fundraiser is not equipped to demonstrate institutional agency in an area that a prospect cares about.

- Conducting research to determine if there is the potential for alignment of institutional capabilities to prospects' purposes.

- Initiating contact in a listening mode, either in the form of an interpersonal interview or an interactive group session, to test and flesh out the potential for alignment.

- Avoiding touting institutional aspirations that do not relate to revealed or established donors' interests.

- Placing more emphasis on evidence of current and project impact and less on promotional platitudes, catchy phrases, or grandiose claims in all materials presented to prospects.

- Creating an institutional ethic that places a far higher value on forming partnerships than getting one-time gifts and, in so doing, committing to creating the climate, the constructs, and the means of collaboration to advance the former and mitigate the latter.

There will always be institutional cultures, or part of them, in which appeals to tribalism will produce a certain amount of gift revenue for certain period of time – but such appeals will not bring out the best in any community, the true philanthropists. True philanthropy is not about money nor amounts given. It is not a gift from the rich, nor noblesse oblige. It exists in all places and all levels of society. It is the clear-eyed conviction that sacrificing a measure of one's individuality is a worthy investment in a world more worthy of vesting one's self in.

Donors do not want to be a factoid in fundraising reports. They want to be more than red mercury in campaign thermometers. They want to live a life of purpose. They want to make a difference. Therefore, they want institutions to be specific about what they intend to achieve and how much it will take. Institutions that give them what they want will achieve and sustain fundraising success.

Yet, great gaps exist between what many institutions hope for from their donors – and what donors want from institutions they support. The inability of institutions to hear and heed their donors wishes can be seen in abundance, perhaps no more so than in the ongoing launch of traditional campaigns, an increasingly false and needlessly expensive exercise now teetering on dated, if not completely false, assumptions. These campaigns will not come close to optimizing institutions' fundraising potential because of the growing gap between what the institution wants for itself and what the philanthropic marketplace is inclined to support. When institutions build their aspirations on what they hope donors will do (notwithstanding evidence of contrary philanthropic interests, behaviors, and patterns) or, more bluntly, simply lose touch with philanthropic realities, they diminish the appeal of that proposed compact and erode their relevance in that society.

Those of us who are actually listening to donors, actually hearing and respecting what they have to say and comparing to institutional behaviors, see the absurdities piling up, including:

- Believing that a campaign will cause donors to be more generous or will attract new donors when objective evidence emphasizes the contrary.

- Cases of support built on the flimsiest of "strategic plans" that never factored in external threats and opportunities, current and emerging, and were not developed from extended listening exercises with key constituents or even vetted with critical stakeholders including estate givers and their most generous and loyal generous donors.

- Placing too much emphasis on catch phrases and graphic design elements, as if they have anything to do with motivating a donor to give, yes, even at the subconscious level.

- Assuming there are lots of donors who will be moved by the call for "leadership gifts" when, in fact, they are asking for institutions to provide evidence that they are providing leadership in some area of human endeavor that warrants their consideration.

- Tons of money being spent on generic "collateral material" that has some small appeal to small tribal elements within that culture but is singularly ineffective in raising funds because it is so generic, so similar to so many other institutions' promotions and so ineffective in engaging donors according to their interests.

- Spending massive sums and going to great lengths to produce splashing public launch events – in which staff usually constitutes the vast majority of attendees.

- Believing they have a "public" who will emerge eagerly from the edge of some forest when they declare themselves in a "public" phase.

So, let's be real. These thoughts *never* occur to donors:

> "I can't wait for the public phase of that campaign to start so I can finally give."
>
> "I think we should give $25,000 to fill in one of those slots on their donor pyramid."

> "I had no interest in giving until they redesigned their logo."
>
> "I'm not going to give them a cent until they develop a stronger social media presence."
>
> "I'm ready to give if they ask me just one more time."
>
> "I hope they'll ask me for a gift far larger than my capacity to give. That will mean that they think I'm really rich!"

Yet, despite their utter improbability, so many organizations continue to assume and act as if such thoughts exist in great store. We need to take our donors' deepest philanthropic convictions far more seriously — and our tactical assumptions much less so.

Let's be more honest with ourselves, starting with facts that are too rarely acknowledged including:

- Most fundraisers can't secure appointments with most of the donors in their portfolios.

- Most of those that can secure appointments struggle with establishing the reason for a second appointment.

- Most institutions lose the largest amounts of donors after one year of giving.

- Most fundraising material fails to impress most managed prospects.

- Most performance metrics don't improve fundraising results.

Therefore, we can safely conclude that most donor acquisition techniques employed by most institutions are increasingly ineffective. The days of deploying generic fundraisers with generic material to scoop up commitments from unquestioningly loyal donors are gone. The old path is eroding past and a much more certain way forward is emerging that anyone with a glimmer of objectivity can see.

In the next chapter we will describe:

- What it takes to build a more philanthropically attuned and responsive culture, including the roles and responsibilities of each level of leadership.

- What the best donors and the best fundraisers have in common and what many institutions are doing to sub-optimize their potential.

- How more donors are seeking ways to give through, rather than give to, institutions.

- How to formulate and broker high impact initiatives that will have much stronger donor appeal.

- How to move beyond traditional fundraising concepts and languages that are proving less and less effective.

CHAPTER 9
BUILDING A MORE ATTUNED AND RESPONSIVE CULTURE

Attuned and responsive cultures know, as W.B. Yeats said, "all's changed, changed utterly." They know the assumptive ships of the past have hit an iceberg of new realities. They squint to see the far shore of possibility and mission fulfillment but keep rowing, rowing, rowing toward it.

REFLECTIVE CULTURE	ASSUMPTIVE CULTURE
Acquires donors by listening to and aligning with their hopes	Acquires donors through rapid, impersonal means
Develops partnerships of enduring purpose	Attempts to reacquire them every year using the same means
Ascertains levels of donor satisfaction	Keeps touting their accomplishments
Makes stewardship an institutional ethic	Thinks of stewardship as tactical advancement function
Offers mission-critical engagement opportunities	Uses advisory boards to stage dog and pony shows
Deepens affinity by responding with the "why" of giving	Doesn't know where it ranks in its donors' philanthropic priorities
Seeks reinvestment based on previous and projected societal ROI	Does little to understand or repair donor loss
Believes you get what you earn	Assumes there's always more

Board members, administrative and academic leaders, and advancement professionals who hope to increase their institutions' fundraising ability must, as the first order of business, commit themselves to learning more about actual, not imagined, philanthropic behaviors, both at the macro level and within their own current and aspirational philanthropic communities.

The most obvious and basic step in that direction is to realize how much opportunity is lost when an institution becomes too consumed with annual fundraising goals, particularly if it subordinates fundraising to balancing the budget, raising a certain amount of unrestricted income or unrestricted endowments. Institutional leaders can no longer think about how much they want and in what form – any more than assuming that the job of fundraising is to get people to give according to broad institutional purposes.

COMMON CHARACTERISTICS	COMMON EXPECTATIONS OF THEM
Animated by ideals and values	Be motivated by annual fundraising goals
Desire to build a better society	Keep an organization afloat
Engaged in authentic problem solving	Transact on tactical operational concerns
Deliberate over substantive studies or practical business plans	Work from grandiose claims, hinting at indirect societal impact
Engage in iterative, progressive dialogue	Reach resolution in a rushed, often awkward way
Dealing in truthfulness, knowing no organization is perfect	Pretend the institution in question has no warts
Uncomfortable with "schmooze and ambush" fundraising	Play mythical, stereotypical parts
Work in ongoing partnership	Move on to the next transaction

The Future of Fundraising

As the preceding chart demonstrates, good donors and good fundraisers have much in common.

Institutions seeking to retain both would be wise, then, to put meaning back into fundraising by adopting a model like this:

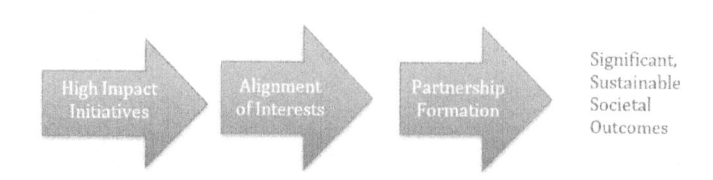

High Impact Initiatives → Alignment of Interests → Partnership Formation → Significant, Sustainable Societal Outcomes

This model is a subset of the larger "purpose-driven model" presented earlier, representing just the portion focused on fundraising. The vast majority of donors today are not interested in providing unquestioning support to institutions to be allocated according to the president's or dean's discretion. They are looking for which institutions they can give through to achieve societal outcomes that respond to, and resonate with, their values and purposes. Examples might include:

- A successful businesswoman giving through the business school she thinks will do the best job of attracting, educating, and empowering future female business leaders.

- An accomplished architect giving through a university, school, or college that he feels best models and provides opportunities for cross-disciplinary student teams to imagine and construct eco-friendly structures that have high aesthetic standards.

- A couple, both M.D.s, giving through a school of public health to help developing countries identify and ameliorate areas prone to outbreaks of epidemics.

- A venture capitalist who made her fortune in the early days of the digital revolution giving through the school that she feels is most committed to bringing the internet to that nation's most technologically underserved areas.

Yet, all those who give through colleges and universities might not always think in such sweeping or large-scale terms. That list could include:

- A Vietnam veteran giving to a local school that has attracted, retained, and graduated the largest number of veterans of recent wars.

- A book collector giving rare 15th and 16th Century legal texts to a local university whose law school and history department collaborated to create a degree program in the history of law.

- A long-married couple who met while working as missionaries in Uganda giving scholarship support to assist students choosing to spend a semester in Africa.

- A Holocaust survivor who gives through a college to help its library build a collection of memoirs, diaries, and memorabilia from other Holocaust survivors.

Other donors may be even more practical in their orientation by directing their giving to academic programs that best anticipate and respond to workforce needs, lead to improved business practices, or promote local economic development.

The Future of Fundraising

Yet, in each instance, we see donors using philanthropy as the vehicle to pass on what life has taught them to be important to current and future generations – and selecting institutions they think are best equipped to do so. They are not institutional supporters. They will not respond to broad institutional appeals but, if listened to and provided an outlet for their lives' passions, can become very generous, repeat donors. They will be drawn to colleges and universities not through institutional promotions or broad events but the ability of institutions to advertise a range of specific, high-impact initiatives led by purpose-driven leaders who demonstrate the potential for converting private support into significant, sustainable societal impact.

The "right institutional outlook," as depicted earlier, will attract and retain these kinds of donors, who represent the rising tide of significant philanthropy. The more rapidly donors are acquired through impersonal means, such as those used in annual funds, the more rapidly they lapse. Those acquired through more personal and substantive means are retained at far higher levels, and the institution delivers on the promises it made to them.

Let's look at each phase of the "impact model" to see how teamwork will lead to superior outcome in each and all.

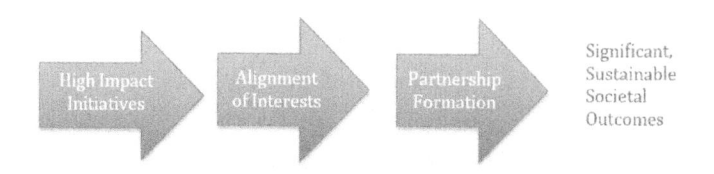

High Impact Initiatives → Alignment of Interests → Partnership Formation → Significant, Sustainable Societal Outcomes

James M. Langley

High Impact Initiatives

It is vital that colleges and universities become proficient at framing high impact initiatives because fundraising, like every other product and service, must adapt to an increasingly segmented philanthropic market. No institution can afford to rely on a single case for support, even if it has multiple options, given the degree of segmentation. Are you presenting your organization like the diner, struggling to stay open, by offering only coffee by the cup or channeling your inner barista to make sure your core services are customized to appeal to a wide variety of philanthropic interests? Please note how those that offer the highest degrees of customization have the longest lines and the fewest open tables.

The only legitimate use for a case for support – or boilerplate language describing the distinguishing characteristics of university, college, school, department, or division – is as an embedment in all documents describing all initiatives. In other words, in this new world, we no longer put one case of support in front of all donors. We put customized initiatives in front of donors and donor groups with longstanding interests in those areas. A donor who has funded only science programs would receive a white paper or proposal customized to that interest. A donor who has given to arts only would receive material that spoke to that passion. Yet, in both, there would be boilerplate language about the College of Arts and Sciences or the university. Whereas once we led with the universal case and followed with specific options, we know must lead with the specific and tuck in the universal thread.

This new ethos in which universities, colleges, schools, departments, and divisions no longer begin conversations about societal impacts that align with preexisting donor interests will also have far greater appeal to alumni. While the vast majority of alumni have continued to gravitate away from their alma maters, because "the only time they reach out to me is when they want money," many might be willing to reengage if they were attracted to a specific initiative driving toward a specific sustainable outcome, especially if that outcome corresponded to their field as a student, their most satisfying extracurricular activity, greatest passion, and/or career interest and made use of their talents and experience. The dollar-driven Venus flytrap model is replaced with one that invites alumni to give of their time and talent to pursue societal outcomes they believe are most important. When people feel good about how their time and talent is being used, treasure follows naturally and often of their own accord. When we seek to drive people to institutional goals, they are reluctant to give us time, see no application for their talents, and resent being asked to give over and over again.

Alignment of Interests

Most fundraising, in particular that which leads to the largest gifts and reinvestments, is not really about one person raising a gift from the other. It is much more like dating in which two people explore shared interests and the potential for spending more time together in the hopes that it will lead to lasting partnership. Indeed, and ironically, the very best fundraisers do not see themselves as mere "fundraisers." They see themselves as professionals who help frame agreements between institutional doers and philanthropic investors. They do this by identifying philanthropists with strong track records of investing in areas that correspond with the strengths of their institutions. They signal to each investor that they are in the business of brokering partnerships of shared purpose. They demonstrate good faith by listening closely to prospects to discern the nature of the life's quest and the role that philanthropy plays in it. When they see partnership potential, they put forward a prospectus or white paper that delineates how specific levels of investment can leverage specific institutional strengths to produce significant, sustainable societal returns. They negotiate their way to common ground, taking as many months as are necessary to establish trust and create the basis of a lasting agreement. When they succeed, they come away with so much more than "a gift." We can see, then, the potential for raising far more money if institutional leaders adopted this outlook and recruited and trained advancement professionals to these purposes.

Partnership Formation

The impact model, at this stage, is not just about securing gifts but creating lasting partnerships of shared purpose. As we saw in the case study of Ms. Lemieux, impact-oriented institutions do not seek to close gifts at the first opportunity (as when she asked, "How can I help?) but to advance an iterative, interactive process which creates a strong alignment of interests. Once formed, these alignments lead to repeated and often increased investments. In other words, this more deliberative and collaborative approach enhances an institution's ability to sustain and increase its levels of private support with every passing year.

When the impact model is employed, colleges and universities are able to retain more donors, because more donors have been acquired not on the basis of what the institution wants them to do for it but on what the institution can do to advance what they care most about. Even more importantly, the impact model helps retain and lift the sights of the most likely source of support, current donors. Yes, loyal donors, by definition and by nature, are more retainable. Every time they make another consecutive annual gift, they become easier to retain. In other words, donor attrition rates decline as years of loyal giving increase, even when institutions don't do anything extraordinary to recognize, retain, or reward loyal giving. Once humans form habits, they are unlikely to change. Therefore, the best predictor of what we will do or how we will behave in the future is what we have done or how we have behaved in the past. That's very good news for institutions that have rafts of loyal donors, especially and remarkably if those habits of loyalty are evinced in every generation after the Greatest and the Boomers. That's very bad news for institutions who have weak patterns of loyalty among the Greatest Generation and the Boomers and ever weaker patterns with ensuing generations – which describes the vast majority of institutions of higher learning in the United States. It is this majority that needs to turn away most quickly from the Venus flytrap model, one of the major contributors to the erosion of institutional loyalty, and more rapidly to the impact model which builds institutional loyalty by interweaving it with enlightened individual interests.

Adoption of the impact model enhances all modes of fundraising, including the one built around the field's two deadliest words:

1. Annual
2. Fund

The first word suggests one give simply because the earth rotated around the sun, again. The second offers only a big bucket from which allocations will be made at some later date for broad institutional purposes.

We must accept the fact that fewer people are willing to give to an institution for the good it has done, and far more are inclined to give through an institution for the good it might do - if described in the form of specific societal outcomes. The latter can be achieved by proposing 5-7 "impact tracks," thereby allowing donors to choose the one that most resonates with their philanthropic priorities — which, by the way, can be the same as the high impact initiatives put in front of major donors. In this way, gifts of all sizes improve the chances of projected outcomes being reached and, if reached, allow every donor to understand the impact of their giving. This approach lifts the sights of loyalists, promotes acquisition of more discerning, purpose-driven donors, and, with effective stewardship, leads to higher donor retention rates for both.

The Future of Fundraising

Once the annual fund has been converted from a begging bowl or a bland buffet of unrelated giving options, institutions can breathe new life into the next most deadly concepts in fundraising:

1. Planned
2. Giving

When used in combination, they are based on the assumptions that:

- Donors, and even some non-donors, will be increasingly inclined to crystalize their giving intentions as decades unfold.
- They will be more inclined to do so, and likely give without restriction, if they are made aware of all the giving options and tax benefits available to them.

These assumptions are misguided, in that:

- The onset of age rarely spurs the non-philanthropic to become philanthropic.
- The philanthropic are motivated far more to life-guiding purposes than by the opportunity to make money on their giving or to achieve tax breaks from it.
- Some 90% of those who leave some or all of their estates to higher education do so in the form of a simple will.
- Donors will give the most to the purposes their lives have taught them to be most important.

Therefore, this function we have called "planned giving" or "estate giving" has over-emphasized the significance of age and financial planning as primary motivating factors, while largely understating the far more important factors including how a life's journey informs and enlivens philanthropic thinking late in life, and how donors imagine giving after death to preserve or pass on to future generations what they discovered was most valuable in theirs.

Once again, the impact model, offers more attractive options for donors thinking about their estates in that it offers the various purpose-driven tracks and therefore more outlets for various specific philanthropic interests, optimizing their giving potential but causing them to think not just about "leaving money" but making lasting differences. This, then, increases the chances of donors thinking about the differences they could make if they thought about a combination of current giving and estate giving. Loyal donors who have given for two decades or more are among the most likely estate givers. They often develop a deep affinity for the institution and, as in the case of many faculty members who become estate givers, are more influenced by institutional priorities. However, the impact model has the potential for raising their philanthropic sights where traditional planned giving programs have little appeal to purpose-driven donors who are not institutional loyalists. In other words, loyalists (a declining segment of donors) are apt to review planned giving literature and factor it into their decision-making. But purpose-driven donors (a rising segment) will ignore it or be unaffected by it. Purpose-driven donors make decisions on the basis of institutional agency not loyalty; therefore, they can come over to an institution late in life if and when they see it as being the most capable of advancing the purpose they deem most important. Indeed, that phenomenon is becoming more common.

All institutions with any semblance of donor loyalty can extend years of loyal giving and increase the amounts given by loyal donors by adopting the impact model. Ms. Lemieux is a classic example. She was a "nice" loyal annual donor, but her giving potential was sub-optimized for many years. Since she gave only small annual gifts and modest special gifts, the AU staff made a fatal assumption – that was all she was capable of or interested in doing. Therefore, they made no effort to further explore her interest and develop her potential. There are many such donors in the ranks of many institution's loyal donors. Like Ms. Lemieux, they have the potential for giving larger annual gifts, major gifts, estate gifts and the blending of all those – if their passion is discovered and aligned with impact-oriented institutional initiatives. This is what the most adept and creative frontline fundraisers have figured out for themselves, even when it was not understood, appreciated, or reinforced by the institutions they represented.

But consider for a moment when the potential of the Ms. Lemieux's of the world are seen. If that researcher had not seen the pattern to her giving, if the vice president and others were not willing to test that thesis, if the right dean with the right idea had not come along, would Ms. Lemieux have persisted in loyal giving? The data suggests that was highly likely. Would she have left a large estate gift? Chances are she might have left a modest estate gift but not a large one. How do we know that? There is no greater predictor of estate giving than loyal giving; the greater the number of years of giving, especially consecutive giving, the higher probability of estate giving.

But wait, did we forget that Ms. Lemieux was also giving to her alma mater and likely other institutions as well? Why would we assume that? Because the Ms. Lemieux's of the world give to 3-5 institutions. If all of them are the beneficiaries of her loyal annual giving, which is most apt to be the recipient of her largest estate commitment? It will be the one that engages her around her strongest philanthropic propensities and produces the greatest, most sustainable societal return on her philanthropic investment.

This is what we see in feasibility studies over and over again. When asked to interview an institution's top donors, we urge that that list of donors be composed primarily of those with the longest patterns of loyal giving, as well as deepest engagement, especially recent engagement. The list of donors that clients turn over for us to interview is composed of donors or prospects that they are convinced are their very best prospects – and theirs alone. Indeed, those donors often come across as quite fond of the institutions we are representing. One would think their future support is all but inevitable until we ask, "Where does this institution stand in your overall philanthropic priorities?" Rarely is the answer: "Number one." In fact, if 25% of any prospect pool of feasibility study interviews answered that way, it would be quite an accomplishment. Donors might answer by saying "somewhere between fifth and seventh" or "in my second tier." Our clients are sometimes crushed to hear that news.

Many institutions have the potential of moving up on their donors' list but do not because:

- They take too much for granted from their giving record alone.

- They fail to discover the "deep why" or the strongest philanthropic motivator, which can be rooted in personal experience, sometimes searing, or in the most important lessons their life has taught them.

- They assume that profuse thanks or recognition is what donors want most.

- They have not customized their fundraising requests to resonate with their donors' most deeply held values.

The most effective fundraising institutions in the future will be those that best hear and heed their constituents, which is not the same as accepting and acceding the demands of the unreasonable. However, it's all too easy to dismiss legitimate complaints as unreasonable. As many a savvy fundraiser and stewardship officer will attest, some of the best gifts come from constructive complainers. They complain because they:

- Hold themselves to high standards, and expect others to do the same.

- Believe in, and hold out hope for, your organization but are disappointed by specific actions or decisions.

- Are results-oriented and don't see you making sufficient progress toward mission milestones.

Yet, too many organizations write off demanding personalities as soreheads or dismiss them as being "in the minority." Yet isn't it always the "demanding minority" that makes the greatest difference in all walks of life? Intuitive professionals, on the other hand, listen, identify with the source of frustration, and propose solutions. When they do, constructive complainers feel heard, respected, validated, reassured, and grateful. When they see organizations stepping up and correcting their course, they put their money where their mouth is, often in a big way.

Being more attuned to such opportunities should cause institutional leaders to rethink what they are looking for in fundraisers – including all those who will take on significant fundraising responsibilities such as presidents, deans, department heads, select administrative leaders, and others. Once again, they must seek to narrow the gap between what institutions have looked for traditionally in fundraisers and what donors are looking for, as the following chart delineates.

WHAT MANY ORGS LOOK FOR	WHAT MANY DONORS LOOK FOR
Rah-rah promoters	Honest depicters of org's strengths and weaknesses
Eager askers	Respectful listeners
Mastery of selling points	Desire to understand donors' motivations
Lone wolf road warriors	Facilitators of multi-faceted engagement
Buoyant personalities	Authentic, accountable agents of philanthropy
Productive pickers of "low hanging fruit"	Patient partnership producers
Closers	Follow through
Those who will "educate" donors over time as to ongoing organizational need	Demonstrators of organizational impact

The Future of Fundraising

The purpose-driven model calls for a fundamental rethinking of what it means to be a fundraiser. It suggests institutions will have to hire fundraisers that look much more like what donors are looking for and equip and train them to be content brokers. In addition, it suggests that boards will have to look for a broader range of qualities in those they choose to be presidents – not just a charismatic, pleasant, or persuasive person capable of charming or schmoozing donors and bringing enough back home to keep the faculty happy. They will need to find leaders with the ability to:

- Inventory institutional assets and determine which can be leveraged to meet current and emerging societal needs.

- Identify academic and administrative leaders who will be able to not only champion an idea but to convert it into a plan that projects ambitious but attainable outcomes, then see those plans through.

- Inform campus constituencies and stakeholders of the competitive challenges to be faced and reposition fundraising not as a reward system for what has been done but as an investment in what could be done to render a greater service to society.

- Imbue a deeper sense of accountability into their cultures by defining how that institution can:
    - Make itself more relevant to its service area and more responsive to the hopes and aspirations of its constituents.
    - Propound substantive concepts that are more worthy of philanthropic consideration.

- o Accept donor stewardship as a collective ethic and shared responsibility.
- o Assess, in open and objective ways what it can do – in the short-, mid- and long-term - to engender appreciation, deepen affiliation, demonstrate agency, and embody accountability.

Indeed, institutions that do the best job of adapting to new philanthropic realities will look more and less like what is depicted below:

MORE	LESS
Stewardship officers	Frontline fundraisers
Stewardship officers carrying larger portfolios	Fundraisers carrying large portfolios
Creating a constituent first, a prospect later	Trying to acquire donors who are not constituents
Thinking of prospects as those with proven mission affinity	Thinking of prospects as wealthy people with potential affinity
Content champions serving as prospect's first point of contact	Deploying frontline fundraisers to initiate new prospect contact
More purpose-driven conversations with prospects	Fewer large events designed to attract prospects
Exploring potential alignments of interests with prospects	Selling prospects on institutional achievements
Gift commitments culminating from progressive conversations	Solicitations staged to present an organization's wants or needs
Mutually obligatory agreements	Pledge forms

The Future of Fundraising

Most institutions have a long way to go to become truly responsive cultures. The most common and significant barriers include:

- Boards reviewing the wrong performance measures (counting the annual yield of fruit in the bushel basket but not asking about the health of the trees or the overall state of the orchard) and drawing the wrong inferences from them which usually results in clamoring for a more aggressive use of bad, inefficient, unsustainable, and, in some cases, philanthropy-depleting fundraising practices.

- Presidents who gain their positions, in part, without acknowledging their lack of fundraising knowledge, doing too little to bone up on it assuming its easily done, or by overstating their fundraising chops, overtly buying into false or simplistic theories of fundraising advanced by board members, faculty, and others – then visiting unrealistic assumptions on their advancement operation.

- Institutional leaders who expect fundraisers to be held to high performance standards but do not apply the same principle to the academic and administrative units that those doing the fundraising represent.

- Chief advancement officers who ply pet theories rather than conduct research on donor psychology and philanthropic behaviors or seek objective assessments of their performance.

- A widespread belief among faculty that donors will reward them for their good work if those donors are sufficiently informed and, in some cases, that donors

- Thinking of, and treating, advancement as a hand-off function and not comprehending where shared responsibilities are crucial to higher functioning: e.g., "Here's what we want, go get it. Isn't that what you people do?" "Alumni relations – your job, we're too busy." "Stewardship – what do you mean I have to account for how the money was used!" "Why do I need to file a donor contact report?" "How do I know you won't use it to steal my donor?"

While each of those barriers may prove difficult to reduce, or even address directly because they are so embedded in the culture, all of them will be more readily seen and acknowledged by most as impediments by adopting the purpose-driven model and explaining and fostering the cross-institutional collaborations necessary to make it come alive.

In the next chapter we will:

- Explain why acquiring constituents has become a prerequisite for acquiring prospects.
- Offer ways of building constituency.
- Enumerate keys to strengthening alumni constituency.
- Provide a case study on constituent engagement.

CHAPTER 10
ACQUIRING CONSTITUENTS

Now we come full circle. We have established that philanthropy is:

1. An outgrowth of the good deeds done by an institution and the seeds of appreciation or admiration they engender, which can be then...

2. Nurtured by experiences and interactions between prospective donors and institutional thought leaders so as to cause those seeds to ripen in philanthropic minds, then...

3. Converted into philanthropic buds when an individual prospect sees, or is presented with, a plan explaining how an institution's good deeds could be expanded or extended to new persons or populations that he or she cares most deeply about, or be transferred without to generate a greater societal impact (economic, cultural, or social), then...

4. Ripened and yielded after negotiations between institutional representatives and the prospect conclude in a gift agreement, then...

5. Regenerated when investments prove productive.

The first, the engendering of good will and appreciation through good deeds has been touched upon, but a further and fuller explication of that phenomenon is beyond the scope of this book. The third, fourth, and fifth have been delineated in detail but the second – whether we call it engagement, affiliation, or constituency building – requires further attention. This is because more and more donors, especially younger ones, are making their giving contingent on active, substantive, participative engagement in any initiative that they might be asked to fund and because the relative absence or weakness of it has become a very real strategic vulnerability for many institutions.

Many institutions these days can be likened to a church, or a civic or cultural organization, that continues to raise respectable amounts of private support each year while acknowledging, each year, "dollars up, donors down." The institution persists but with few middle-aged or young donors in its pews or seats. It becomes clear that that status is unsustainable. Even if the game never runs out completely and the institution manages to survive, it becomes less relevant. It becomes a preserved institution not a living institution. More vibrant, more relevant, more contributory, more sustainable institutions need more middle aged and younger donors in their pews or seats. And to do that, they have to draw people to those pews and seats by offering something that is interesting and fulfilling for them. In short, they can't expect to attract and sustain strong levels of private support without first building a stronger congregation, constituency, or community, then demonstrating agency – or the ability to make a difference in ways that are most satisfying, if not inspiring, to their members and to the larger communities they serve.

Institutions can't turn constituency building over to fundraisers. Would any of us be inclined to join a church, social club, or cultural organization if recruited only by a fundraiser, no matter how nice that person might be? How might we feel if every time we went to that institution we were greeted by a fundraiser, saw fundraisers in every pew, row, or table and spent most of our time there hearing about fundraising needs? How would we feel if we were encouraged to get more engaged – but only by a fundraiser? Would we not conclude we were being offered only highly conditional love? Would anything in those experiences make us feel valued for who we are or for whatever talent we could bring to bear on mission realization?

The best ways to build constituency are to:

- Offer people what they can't get elsewhere (they can get galas and golf tournaments anywhere).
- Provide experiences that money can't buy.
- Offer people outlets for the passions and worthy application of their talents.
- Show them how they continue to make a difference, individually and collectively.
- Share how even greater differences can be made.

Then money will come. It will come without arm-twisting, endless asking, whining, or wheedling. Yet without greater attention paid to constituency building as depicted above, fundraising will prove more and more difficult and success will continue to be marked by fundraiser totals propped up by fewer, wealthy, aging donors. Contrary to a fairly common myth out there, generations after Baby Boomers will not begin to behave like Boomers when they reach a certain age and become more generous, more loyal, and more unquestioning. If we study human behavior through any lens, we see most of us are creatures of habits. Once formed, habits persist. The longer they persist, the more they harden. The very best predictor of what post Boomers will do tomorrow is what they are doing today. Institutions will either meet them where they are or be left behind by them.

And the constituency that most institutions simply must do a better job with is their alumni. They must acknowledge that students will not become participative alumni if they did not feel themselves the beneficiaries of:

- A system (as opposed to a few teachers, coaches, or staff members) designed to develop their potential.
- Caring guidance through that system.
- Learning experiences that could not be had elsewhere.
- A door-opening diploma that proved its value as being far greater than the cost.

Further, they will be less likely to sustain alumni participation if the appreciation for them doesn't deepen with time and if the institution doesn't engage them as equals, showing where their talent and time can be best applied to extend similar institutional benefits to current and future students and to otherwise make differences that society most needs and wants.

Most institutional leaders are a long way from the realization of what it really takes to produce participative alumni. They too often assume that their advancement or alumni relations will turn former students with very uneven experiences into a rabid, rah-rah tribe clamoring for more opportunities to come back, look back, and give back. It's not working. And the less inclined institutions are to listen to their students, to explore gaps between what they hope for upon enrollment and what they are experiencing now, the less likely they are to attempt to correct the course before those students leave or graduate. The less inclined they are to listen to alumni about the strengths and weaknesses of the student experience, the less inclined their alumni will be to believe that their experience mattered and that their alma mater is determined to learn from the past so that it can better serve the needs of the present and the future. The less alumni feel they matter, either for what they learned from the past or what they can offer to building a better future, the less likely they are to be engaged, to find any utility in attending homecomings, reunions, regional events, or the slate of usual alumni offerings. And the more present and persistent fundraising is – in, around, or at these events – the more likely alumni are to fall away from them or avoid them altogether.

So many learning institutions claim to have imparted "critical thinking" skills to their students but treat their alumni as if they had none. They communicate with their alumni as if they were all rabid boosters and offer engagement opportunities that appeal only to those with too much time on their hands. Many critical-thinking alumni look at both and conclude, "It's all a ruse for fundraising. They're trying to sweet talk me into a pastry tube – and think I don't see the squeeze coming." No, they may not think in such sarcastic terms, but they come to the same conclusion. That's why most institutions interact with less than 10% of their total alumni populations, why they consider an event attended by more than 100 alumni as a roaring success, and why alumni annual giving has declined for 30 years, and why alumni no longer constitute the largest source of private support for higher education.

Squeezing alumni with very different students' experiences, career interests, and worldviews for more money to support broad purposes and processes doesn't just result in poor fundraising results. It diminishes positive word of mouth among alumni that can enhance institutional reputation, influence student recruitment, strengthen employer interest, and cause institutions to be seen in their communities as valued partners.

While realizing the greater ideal of building educational systems that engender greater student appreciation and alumni affiliation takes time and assiduous attention, institutions can send much more positive signals, particularly to their most conscientious and accomplished alumni, by advertising a series of initiatives designed to leverage institutional strengths so that it might better serve large societal interests – and thereby strengthen the students experience, enrich alumni engagement, and create a stronger community of shared purposes. Those initiatives could be driving toward impact in all sorts of areas, such as those enumerated in Chapter Seven. Let's imagine how it might look for an imaginary university.

Under the new leadership of its innovative president, and with the active participation of campus stakeholders, Imaginary

THE FUTURE OF FUNDRAISING

University announces its "Dare to Make A Difference" plan. The areas in which it has decided it can make the greatest difference are:

Converting Demographic Realities into Regional Advantages. The goal is to create a more seamless educational system in which all participating parties work on improving the persistence of all students, including conducting research as to which methods work best with distinct ethnic populations so that the whole can be advanced as series of distinct but complementary educational tracts.

Creating More Advantages for the Aging By Capitalizing on the Advantage of Aging. The goal is to recruit a cadre of accomplished people over the age of 60 to help identify where the aging are struggling and develop alleviative strategies, identify under-used talents possessed by members of their cohort and link them to the needs of nonprofits, and develop a curriculum for those interested in learning how to make the most of their stage of life.

Improving Our Collective Mental Health. The goal is to redefine mental health as a community asset, to assess its current state as perceived by key sectors and populations segments, identify gateways and barriers to its improvement, and hold up a mirror to the community so that each of us can see how we can better help all of us.

Enriching Our Collective Culture. The goal is to identify various art forms in the community, including those expressed in specific ethnic cultures, and to provide an ongoing showcase for them and ongoing discussion of what makes them unique to a particular culture and what makes them universal.

Each of these initiatives is built on institutional strengths. Each has a "Coordinating Champion." For each of these initiatives, Imaginary University lists desired and optimal outcomes in two years and in five years. Each has a goal in enriching the student experience, in enriching search, and in serving the community.

As more institutions move in the direction of Imaginary University, more alumni, even those with imperfect experiences, are likely to take pride in their alma maters for stepping up to the big issues of the day, more alumni will see their purposes and their values reflected in one or more of the initiatives, more will ask how they can "be involved" and more will see their alma mater as a magnet and less of a pastry tube.

The following model suggests how an institution can use the generation of white papers, describing proposed high-impact initiatives to engage constituents across the board.

The Future of Fundraising

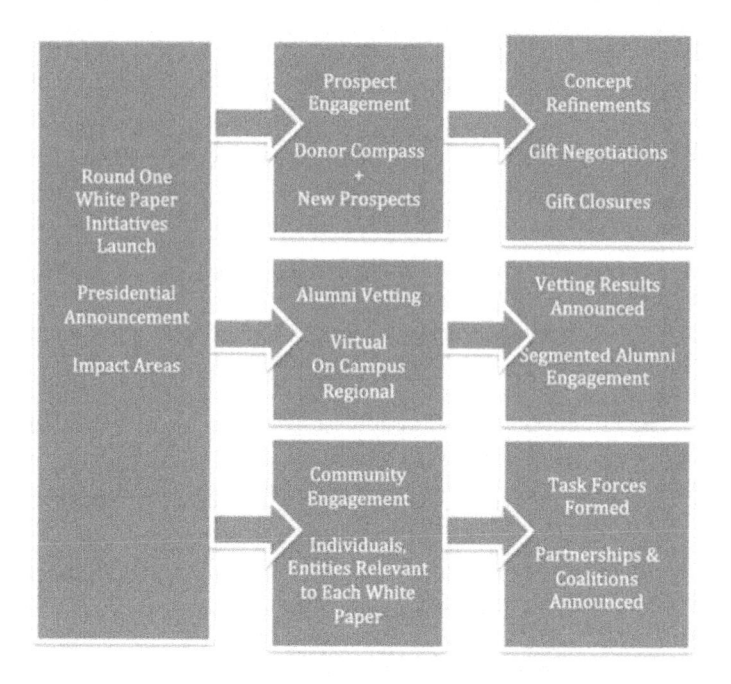

Round One White Paper Initiatives Launch	Prospect Engagement — Donor Compass + New Prospects	Concept Refinements / Gift Negotiations / Gift Closures
Presidential Announcement / Impact Areas	Alumni Vetting — Virtual / On Campus / Regional	Vetting Results Announced / Segmented Alumni Engagement
	Community Engagement — Individuals, Entities Relevant to Each White Paper	Task Forces Formed / Partnerships & Coalitions Announced

The model offers many more opportunities for substantive engagement, depending on alumni appetites for engaging, including:

- Being asked to take part in specific initiative planning sessions.
- Reviewing drafts of proposed initiatives.
- Interacting with "coordinating champions" on campus or at regional events.
- Joining action teams or evaluation teams associated with each initiative.
- Serving as a regional "coordinating champion."

In these and other ways, learning institutions can provide "portals of purpose" and talent-specific engagement opportunities for their most accomplished and conscientious alumni in all walks of life. They can move away from the model that offers only:

- The opportunity to come back, look back, give back.
- Attend nostalgic events like homecoming and reunion.
- Gatherings around athletic events or game watching parts.
- Local chapters of clubs.
- Gathering at alumni centers which are not, literally or figuratively, in the heart of the campus.
- Attend events that tout institutional achievements.

While each of those events or activities have some appeal to some alumni, the totality of offerings is grossly insufficient if institutions are to attract greater alumni notice or to draw and make use of more alumni talent. And the poorer the job an institution does in justifying the time asked of its alumni and in making use of their talents, the less potential it has to be the recipients of their treasure.

Moving from an institutional support model to a purpose-driven model (in which new operational expenses can be consumed) requires institutional leaders to conduct planning processes that identify where and how institutional strengths can be leveraged to make a larger societal difference or perhaps where institution strengths should be built to respond to or capitalize on a larger societal need. This planning would result in the declaration of difference making initiatives as we saw in the case of Imaginary University.

But this book has argued throughout for participative processes to create coalitions of shared purpose and using every important internal deliberation as an opportunity to engage external constituents – which eventually blurs the distinction between the two. Therefore, the creation of signature initiatives should include:

- External needs assessment for the issue or area to be addressed for each initiative.

- The identification of, and consultation with, external entities, including civic leaders and philanthropists who have been addressing the same issue, directly or indirectly.

- The exploration and engagement of other external entities that may be critical in accelerating or slowing the initiative's momentum, including governmental bodies and citizen action groups.

Once the determination has been made as to which initiatives are most promising, and planning bodies are empaneled to begin developing operational plans, attention should be paid to populating those bodies with internal and external members on the basis of merit, with consideration for major donors, loyal donors, and estate donors as well as top volunteer leaders.

When initiative plans are fleshed out (a template for doing so will be provided below), it is important to vet them with both broad constituent groups as well as potential external partners, including those with the potential of underwriting them. After the vetting process, it will become clear which ideas have the strongest external appeal.

To help thought leaders and coordinating champions turn initiative concepts into compelling white papers that can be tested as recommended above, a questionnaire such as this can prove very helpful.

1. *What need or opportunity in the community, or in society, do you seek to address or redress?* Examples: Growing workforce demand, unmet social services, injustice, dampened community potential because of failure to provide opportunity or train segments of the populace, etc.

2. *What proven capabilities does your unit or potential partners have to meet that need or rise to that opportunity?* Examples: Describe the current impact of a particular program, initiative, or service; a thought leader with a strong reputation in the area to be addressed; third party awards, grants, or other validations; etc. (Remember: The more factual, the better.)

3. *Describe the program, service, or initiative you intend to launch or expend to meet this need or expand that opportunity?* (Remember: Keep this section to about 500 words because the purpose of this document is to see if the concept resonates with donors and to start a conversation about how we can work together. Don't

try to wow them into philanthropic submission by using lots of superlatives.)

4. *What will it take to capitalize this initiative?* What's a ballpark estimate for the next stage budget? What resources do you currently have? How are they being expended? Where would private support prove to be most catalytic? How would you expend the first $25k - $100k, the second $25k to $100k, etc.?

5. *What impact do you project if you secure the requisite funding?* Who will benefit? How will they benefit? When will they realize those benefits?

6. *How will you monitor and/or evaluate your progress, and how will you communicate the results to your investors?*

Each institution will determine how many concept papers and signature initiatives are prudent to produce and present. Giving every major academic and administrative unit (e.g., athletics and student affairs) a chance to compete, and to see how they fare in testing mode, is fine, but institutional leaders need to be careful about flooding the market with too many ideas. Instead, it is wise to phase the release of impact initiatives. In that way, no credible concept or champion thereof need feel that the "train has left the station," only that it is not yet the appropriate time to add their car to the train and will draw far more attention to their initiative if they allow other cars to get farther down the track.

There are, of course, all sorts of variations on this approach. Dickinson's president, Margee Ensign, for instance invited alumni, parents, and other external constituents to submit initiative ideas in the name of "co-innovation" under a broader initiative called "The Revolutionary Challenge." Contrary to the prediction of some skeptics, scores of credible ideas poured in, which were then evaluated and scored online, with thousands of alumni participating, and finalists were determined by a blue-ribbon panel of accomplished alumni, faculty, and other stakeholders. The approach was most noteworthy in a number of ways, including the quality of proposals produced, the willingness of many alumni to take the time to review them online, and the institution's ability to attract some its most successful alumni to serve as judges, who, as a result of being an integral part of an innovative and strategic process, then offered to mentor concept champions and underwrite emerging initiatives.

Simon Fraser University (SFU) is testing ideas first as pilot projects floated in their annual giving program – both to secure immediate funding and to see if the concept could be grown into a larger initiative. They recently offered annual donors a new option – student mental health. The result: SFU saw an immediate uptick in alumni participation, especially from younger donors, some of whom may not have given otherwise. The direct mail portion invited alumni to not only provide financial support but to return note cards advising students how to cope with stress. Dozens of alumni responded. One wrote a three-page letter. Those alumni notes were posted where students gather with an invitation to write back to those alumni whose notes most resonated with them. Earlier, the same team offered alumni the opportunity to provide support for students who were single parents. Again, that opportunity resonated strongly with a significant subset of alumni who otherwise might not have been moved to give. Rather than urging many to give to one purpose, SFU is experimenting with seeing how many personal identifiers, like the strands of a rope, can be woven into one ever more responsive organization. That's how they hope to engender more hope, trust, and sustained participation.

In these variations, we still see the constants advocated in this book — most especially that fundraising in the future, if it is to be successful year over year, must be much less about what donors can do for institutions and much more about how doers and donors can work together to imagine and pursue ways they can make differences where differences most need to be made.

Alumni are an institution's most important external constituency. The levels of appreciation, affiliation, and belief in their alma mater's agency are leading indicators of greater success and greater struggle. As institutions become more intentionally purpose-driven and initiative-oriented, they increase the potential and begin the process of building coalitions of shared purpose. As more alumni are engaged in the process and are able to come in through more portals that correspond with their purpose, the more we see the applicability of the model to other constituents including parents and "friends." And the more we see the potential of drawing forward new constituents from many different places who strongly identify with and want to be a part of a particular signature initiative.

Then we see how the organizing principles of one generation become the artificial constructs of the next, why:

- Putting parents in boxes like parent funds and parent programs preempts a greater civic or philanthropic potential by failing to provide a larger portal of purpose that corresponds to their life's animating passion.

- Annual giving strategies, particularly those that offer prospects only funds, are declining in appeal, and why many donors are gravitating to smaller local nonprofits or simply giving off the institutional grid in ways that are more meaningful to them.

- Planned giving has been consigned too often to finalizing gift agreements before people die while failing to awaken those donors' deeper philanthropic instincts and inspire them to think about the right combination of outright and deferred giving to advance the purpose nearest and dearest to them, and why planned giving instruments, when offered as an end to themselves do not draw forward significant numbers of new donors with or without some current or prior affiliation.

- Cause-oriented donors, which includes many post-Boomers, and those of modest means did not see themselves in institutional offerings and gravitated to small nonprofits and crowd funding options where they could see the difference they could make.

All of which should cause us to see the need for an entirely different philanthropic construct, one that offers impact-oriented purpose, portals, and channels, one that does not seek to organize us by the traditional nomenclature – student, faculty, staff, alumnus, parent, foundation, corporation, or friend – but where we find common cause irrespective of the categories and how we might, as kindred spirits, work together to make a difference that no one of us ever could.

In the next chapter we will:

- Speak to the quality that allows fundraising to be practiced at its highest and most sustainable level – emotional intelligence.

- Demonstrate the power of emotional intelligence when applied to all areas of advancement practice.

James M. Langley

CHAPTER 11
EMOTIONAL INTELLIGENCE

The importance of emotional intelligence in creating more responsive and respectful ways of fundraising cannot be overstated. The absence of it has been and will continue to be damaging to efforts to restore constituent trust and confidence.

The absence of it can be seen in incessant appeals, in efforts to treat the philanthropic compact as one-sided (what you should do for institutions), in ambush asks, in asking for wildly unrealistic amounts, and in other ways that show an inability to listen to donors – before, during, and after solicitations. During the COVID-19 crisis, the presence of it could be seen in those organizations that retreated from explicit fundraising, asked only when there was a clear and pressing need, and used the time to listen to their constituents, reinforce loyalty and build community. The absence of it could be seen in those institutions that did little or none of that activity and in some virtual discussions where advancement professionals asked if fundraising cessation was necessary and if so, how quickly they could return to the status quo. Those were the wrong questions. The far better question would have been: "What must we do today and in the weeks ahead to cause donors to want to give again, as much as they can, whenever they can?"

The answer would not have been a return to the status quo. It would be to stop asking donors to give to their institutions and start showing donors how they can give through them to achieve specific, sustainable societal gains. It would be a growing awareness that institutions have to stop competing as bastions of overhead, each clamoring support to ensure that they continue to exist, and to start collaborating with other entities to make greater differences where differences most need to be made. The institutional support model has been running out of steam and will continue to do so. Institutions that continue to rely on it will find themselves in competition with organizations – more lean, more real, more mission obsessive, and closer to the ground. They will, at some point, have to decide if they want to compete with donors' favored causes or to join forces to help advance them.

[handwritten note: institutional vs impact model]

The point here is that these trends and shifting tendencies are already clear. The lack of adaption to them is not rooted in a lack of intelligence or in a lack of data but in the lack of emotional intelligence in guiding the gathering, analyzing, and applying data – and that may be an overly fancy way of saying that it is really about an insufficient desire or ability to listen to donors, to struggle to understand what they are searching for (indeed they may be struggling with the same), to hear what they are saying at an emotional level, and to find common cause with them.

Those with emotional intelligence understand that institutional relations are simply human relations writ large. They simply apply the precepts of successful interpersonal relationships to their work in constituent relations. To demonstrate how this might work, try your hand at the following:

Let's say you have a circle of friends who once seemed of one mind. Whatever you wanted to do, they wanted to do — or so you thought. However, now when you announce what you want to do, fewer respond, fewer do what you suggest, and more push back with suggestions of their own. Others are much slower in responding and seem less enthusiastic, and still others seem to be ignoring your requests and not responding at all. What do you do?

Ask them more often and more emphatically assuming they missed your earlier requests?

Change your language assuming they will respond better if you use catchier phrases?

Change your appearance so you look hipper and more with the times?

Wrap yourself in more expensive material so they will be more taken with your appearance and therefore assume that you must be more important?

Hire coaches and consultants to make you seem more interesting and appealing?

Attend conferences on human advancement and look for sessions on dealing with non-responsive friends?

Ask your friends to take a survey listing so they can vote on ways they would most like to interact with you?

Ask them to come to a reunion, so you can ask, "What gives?"

> *Ask them to a reunion by previewing that you want to learn how you could be a better friend?*
>
> *Meet with your most loyal friends first and ask them how you could be a better friend?*
>
> *Call your closest friends and ask how they are, using lots of follow-up questions and thereby encouraging them to share?*
>
> *Ask them for what you want as infrequently as possible and only when it corresponds to what they're interested in?*

Perhaps you've chuckled your way through these options, seeing how inapt the earlier options are and how the list moves towards more sensible options that have a far better chance of restoring one's circle of friends. Perhaps along the way, you have found the choices so obvious that you've concluded that you must have a high level of emotional intelligence.

Ah, but here's the rub. Now go back through and substitute "donors" for the word "friends" and ask yourself which of these approaches are closer your institution's approach to donor retention? In too many instances, they look at lot more like the first eight options and too little like the last four. In too many instances, we employ strategies in the name of institutional relations that we would recognize as absurd in interpersonal relations. So, the kind of emotional intelligence that we need more of is that which applies interpersonal wisdom to the framing and application of institutional strategies.

If we are to better understand why donors may have lost faith in our institutions, we must ask ourselves if it might be for the same reasons we lose faith in individuals. If we listened, really listened, as emotionally intelligent individuals and not as institutional shills, might we not hear lost donors feeling as if:

- You are always asking for yourself and never asking what I need.

- When I try to tell you, you nod your head, but I see no evidence that you heard or intend to do anything about what I shared.

- You assume that I am here for you and you alone but you don't seem to see how alone that makes me feel; even when you say you're here for me, I don't see any change in your behavior.

- Our interests are diverging.

- What you are doing and proposing to do seems less and less relevant to me and what I care about.

- Others seem more appreciative, even when I do less for them than I do for you.

- Others tell me how I make a difference; you keep acting as if I haven't done enough, so I keep wondering if it will ever be enough no matter what I do.

When we listen with emotional depth, we can hear in ways that others cannot and respond in ways that others do not. We can build closer relationships. Now let's apply that notion across a range of institutional advancement functions.

The Future of Fundraising

Prospect Engagement

When meeting with prospective donors, do we talk more than we listen? Do we act like a jerk on the first date? To avoid doing so, try this exercise:

> Imagine having met someone who you might want to spend the rest of your life with. You ask him/her out. He/she agrees. On that first date with this potential partner, would you:
>
> *Whip out a brochure or play a video touting your accomplishments and laying out your ambitions?*
>
> *Talk most of the time and steer the conversation back to your dazzling self at every opportunity?*
>
> *Never allude to the future and just be "on the make?"*
>
> *Ask them to commit to anything then and there?*

Skilled practitioners know better. If the first meeting was hopeful, they begin exploring the basis for a second, third, fourth, fifth "date." They commit to a thorough process of mutual discovery, not expecting too much too soon, while developing, delighting in, and reinforcing common interests at as they emerge. Sure, representing an organization in a first donor meeting is a bit different than representing yourself romantically but the same precepts apply. We acquire lifelong donors by applying what life has taught us about building lasting human relationships. And more and more research shows that the most successful major gifts unfold after long courtships of at least a year.

Events

> Ask yourself how likely you would be to attend an invitation from a friend or neighbor if you:
>
> *Think it's a ruse to sell products or has some other hidden agenda.*
>
> *Think all they're offering is an update from the hosts on the wonderful things they're doing and why you should be impressed.*
>
> *Don't feel sentimental and nostalgic about time you spent with your host a long time ago.*
>
> *Find the proposed gathering is not nearly as interesting or enriching as other events on your social calendar.*
>
> *Are not sure if you'll know anyone there and, therefore, find yourself in a socially awkward position.*
>
> *Don't know when it will end and fear getting stuck there for too long.*

The Future of Fundraising

By putting ourselves in the position of the invitees rather than inviters, we can see that many institutions simply assume too much in their event planning. They assume invitees are so loyal or have such deep affinity that they are craving institutional updates full of the latest bragging points, or are so nostalgic that they can't wait to come back, or, even worse, are just dying for a fundraising pitch.

When the emotionally intelligent are engaged in fundraising events, they ask what the event could offer invitees that:

- They couldn't get elsewhere.
- Money couldn't buy.
- Even incredibly busy people would carve out time for.
- Would make them feel complimented to take part in.
- Would give them a role or a purpose, especially one that would showcase their expertise or allow them to lend their wisdom.
- Would leave them wanting more of the same or even deeper engagement.
- Would allow them to interact with kindred spirits.
- Ensure that they won't feel neglected, alone, or wondering why they came.

They don't begin with assumptions about the attendees but seek to create means of engagement that are of mutual benefit and where the hosts can get to know the invitees better not just hold forth on themselves.

JAMES M. LANGLEY

Stewardship

If we think about stewarding human relationships, we think both in terms of ongoing obligations and what we can do to keep those relationships vital over time. In the case of partner relations, we might think of our basic obligations in terms of recognizing and celebrating anniversaries, birthdays, and Valentine's Day, and the importance of being together on key holidays such as Thanksgiving and those linked to our faith. In fact, most stewardship offices will attempt to do the same for their donors, including sending Valentine's Day cards. The emotionally intelligent will ask if the institution enjoys a close enough relationship with some donors to justify sending something like a Valentine's Day card and, if not, if the donor might view such efforts as false, presumptive, disingenuous, or cloying. Further, they will ask if any of those have meaning to donors – if:

- They come from an office, not a person.
- They come from a person, and that person is close to the donor.
- The only person they are hearing from is in the development office.
- Every expression of affection comes across as conditional love.

While meeting obligations is of great importance, much more is required to sustain healthy relationships. For instance, imagine one partner, at a wistful or melancholy moment, saying, "I'm not sure I am as important to you as I once was." Then imagine the other respond by saying, "Now, honey, how can you say that? I remembered your birthday and our anniversary, *and* I gave you roses on Valentine's Day!" That describes a "check the box" approach to relationship management. However, in vibrant relationships, partners do much more than meet obligations to one another. They keep their relationships alive by showing a genuine interest in the other, by communicating and listening in considerate ways, and by offering spontaneous expressions of love and support. Indeed, the moments and memories we are most likely to cherish the longest are the least expected when, perhaps, someone we love tells us how rare, wonderful, important, good, kind, or valuable we are to them – out of the clear blue. Such moments are remembered as the most romantic.

So, the emotionally intelligent will affirm the importance of providing receipts, reports, thank-you's, and other niceties to donors on a regular schedule. They might also advocate and facilitate senior officers, board members, and others in your organization to carry thank-you cards with them, so they can send spontaneous, handwritten notes when they see the impact of philanthropy, such as:

> "I heard a concert last night in the hall named for you. I hope you know how much joy you bring to so many, so regularly."
>
> "The speakers coming to campus as a result of the lecture

> series you have endowed are bringing out record numbers of students and deeply enriching their campus experience."
>
> "I have taught several students that you have supported with scholarships. They would not be here otherwise, and we would be the lesser for it."

Those with EI understand that donors want to hear how their gifts continue to make a difference. It doesn't matter if they know the writers of those kind of notes; such unexpected affirmations, as with all of us, will make a donor's day, and help your organization demonstrate that it believes that stewardship is everyone's business.

In addition, those with EI know that many put more stock in deeds than they do in words, and they suggest ways their institutions can demonstrate how important loyalty and generosity are, by:

- Reserving front row seats, especially at your most prestigious events, for your most loyal donors and recognizing them at the beginning of every program.

- Establishing a policy that no major plan or decision will be considered final before it is vetted with your estate donors and loyalists of 25 years or more.

- Recognizing anniversary dates (5 years, 10 years, etc.) with greater "insider status" – e.g., 5-year donors invited to group strategic consultation with the CEO, 10-year donors invited to dialogue with the president and board, etc.

The Future of Fundraising

As invariably is the case, doing what is right – respecting and recognizing donors for what they have done – proves to be very smart and practical. Most major gifts and major estate gifts come from loyal donors.

Advancement practitioners with high "EQ" understand most new dollars do not come from new donors but from learning something new about the donors they already know. With the decline in individual giving, the rise of impact-oriented philanthropic investors, and donors taking longer to determine where their largest gifts will go, the most important "fundraising" skills will be genuine curiosity, emotional intelligence, psychological acuity, and conscientiousness — all of which will allow organizations to do a far better job of:

- Understanding the most important and inviting questions to ask and knowing how to ask them.
- Grasping what donors are really trying to say and knowing how to respond so that they feel heard.
- Linking pronounced donor passions to distinct organizational capabilities.
- Creating deeply rewarding donor experiences.
- Proving your organization is the place where donors' deepest convictions will be respected and where their greatest hopes will be realized.

Yes, some of us will say that those skills have always been the most essential but, in the coming years, the absence of them will fatal and the sub-optimization of them will prove evermore damaging.

Finally, no one with an ounce of EI would include a request for additional funding to anything done in the name of stewardship or donor relations. When put in interpersonal terms, it seems like saying, "Now that I have given you a birthday card, will you pick up my laundry?"

Controversies/Crisis Management

The emotionally intelligent know that tough times forge the strongest bonds. They understand, therefore, that controversies and crises can be managed in ways that build stronger communities of shared purpose. Where others feel shame when confronted with struggles and setbacks, the emotionally intelligent call on their friends, close the door and say, "I need your help." That's when friends feel trusted, complimented, and valued.

Emotionally intelligent leaders understand the importance of immediate and full disclosure and that the process must start with their closest friends – in this case, their most loyal and generous donors and their most faithful volunteers. When they know bad news about the institution will be breaking in the news media, they call, write, or visit those friends, saying, "I wanted to make sure you heard directly from me or us before you heard it on the news or read it in the paper." Those with EI know when this is done, donors:

- Feel as if they are in the inner circle because of the trust placed in them.

- Interpret the bad news more generously having heard it from "on high."

- Are more likely to offset the impact of it in their spheres of influence, because most people put more stock in the testimony of credible insiders than in media accounts.

- Are more likely to take an active hand in the resolution of the controversy or crisis.

- Are more likely to give notwithstanding the institution's struggles.

In anticipation of the inevitability of such moments, those with EI think about which donors are most important to be visited or otherwise contacted and by whom – and even prepare those lists so they will be ready when the time comes.

Volunteer Recruitment and Management

With the ability to put themselves in the shoes of current and would-be volunteers, those with EI ask themselves: If I were them:

- What would I find most meaningful to do?

- How would I like to be asked and by whom?

- How would I not like to be treated?

- What would frustrate me or cause me to feel devalued?

Knowing that many people, no matter how busy or accomplished, are not only willing to lend their expertise if the right time and place can be worked out but will feel complimented to be asked by an institutional leader, those with EI seek to:

- Identify donors, alumni, parents, and others with exceptional skills that would lend themselves to the mission advancement of the institution or some significant part of it.

- Determine the right person to request it with the understanding that certain protocols matter.

- Identify the recipient of the services to be offered to be sure that the expertise imparted is acted upon and the results of doing so are shared.

- Do everything possible to ensure that volunteer contributions of time and talent are facilitated to make them as convenient and enjoyable as possible.

- Listen to volunteers throughout to make sure they feel as if their time and talent were put to good use.

In addition, they will think about a larger set of volunteer and engagement opportunities that render a real service to the institutions they represent while making good use of volunteers' time and talent. They don't under-estimate the discernment of their volunteers by putting them through hollow exercises as a pretext for fundraising requests. They put real issues, drafts of important plans, and pending decisions in front of those who lend real value to processes of review and refinement, and they listen – at literal, figurative, and emotional levels.

Research

Research seeking to understanding the proclivities of key constituencies or seeking to "predict" those most capable of future giving can easily turn into a rabbit hatch romp, with variables piling on variables until constants become indiscernible. To prevent that from happening emotional intelligence is required in the design of the survey to ask:

- What is most important for us to learn?
- What will we do with what we learn?
- What are the best and most interesting questions that will reveal the most important information?

They seek psychological insight, not to sneak up on donors or bend them to their will, but to ensure they put forward ideas and options that have a strong likelihood of appealing to those donors' interests and resonating with their values. They understand the best indication of what someone will do in the future is what they have done in the past, so they seek to track behaviors over time including four key propensities:

- Philanthropic or not
- Occasionally or consistently

- To various causes and purposes or with a focus on a particular area

- Generosity within their means (which reveals, for instance, that the billionaire who gives hundreds of thousands here and there is less philanthropic than the millionaire who gives $100,000 each and every year)

When gathering oral information, in interviews or focus groups, they listen in various ways knowing that different people expresses themselves in different ways be they literal, figurative, emotional, or various blends. When reviewing written results, emotionally intelligent people seek to read between the lines in an attempt to understand not just what people said or felt, but why.

Prospect Profiles

Individual prospect research seeks to yield the same results as the broad constituent research cited above but with the more explicit purpose of acquiring a new donor or finding something that will resonate more deeply with existing donors. Those with EI know how to use research, for themselves and/or to guide others with prospects and donors, to broker meetings with prospects, to put them at ease, to explore how their interests might align with institutional ambitions, and to discover what kinds of institutional engagements they will find interesting and rewarding.

The Future of Fundraising

Someone with considerable EQ is critical to sustained success of principal and major gifts teams. Such teams should include a researcher, a frontline fundraiser, and a content champion, and high EQ may be found in any of those positions, but at least one member of the team must have it and the others must recognize its indispensability.

So, the next time you are hiring a gift officer or are somehow involved in the search, make sure you don't interview them; ask them to interview you. Develop a one-page profile on a prospect you know well (with the name redacted, of course). Drop some clues about that donor's propensities in that profile but don't paint the whole picture. Give your gift officer candidates 10 minutes to review that profile before asking them to interview you as if you were the prospect in question and the candidate was meeting that donor for the first time. Do they:

- Put you at ease?
- Exhibit natural curiosity and genuine interest?
- Pose questions that explore that donor's value system?
- Propose ways in which your institution could advance those values?
- Create a legitimate rationale for a subsequent meeting?

If one candidate does all those things well, you have strong indicators of considerable emotional intelligence. The only question you need to ask is: "When can you start?"

To make sure those with strong individual skills also have the emotional intelligence to understand the value of working in a team with those who have complementary skills, ask them: "Please describe your greatest fundraising success."

- If they brag about bedazzling the bejesus out of a single prospect, give them a score of 1, if not 0.
- If they speak to the power of patient persistence in working to optimize the philanthropic potential of a prospect, assign a score of 2.
- If they describe helping to create conditions in a particular culture that led to higher, repeated fundraising success, award a score of 3.

Other sample questions:

- What is the most important fundraising lesson you have learned?
- What was your greatest fundraising challenge and how was it resolved?
- What would you like your successor to say about your fundraising record?

Score as follows:

- "Me"-oriented answers = 1. These indicate an egotistical/extractive attitude.
- Any power of process answers = 2. These indicate a realistic/relational approach.

- Any content-rich, conscientious, collaborative answers = 3. These indicate a strategic/sustainable outlook).

Look for those who score lots of 3's or 2's but still speak to the importance of tactical proficiency and disciplined processes. When in doubt, round down. Hire the candidates with the highest total scores. Watch a more successful, sustainable philanthropic culture take root.

There are, of course, various levels of emotional intelligence - the deeper, the rarer. Those levels might be imagined this way:

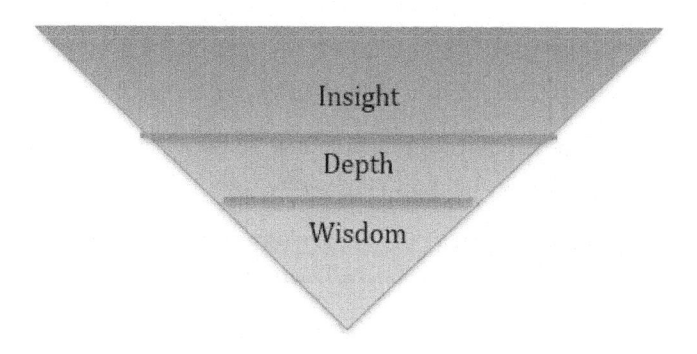

Insight

Depth

Wisdom

These qualities, at any level, are critical for any institution to have in store if they are to preserve the philanthropic body, much less make it more robust. Philanthropy is the manifestation of the best in human nature – a willingness to hold less for ourselves so that we might do more for those less fortunate or for a greater collective good. It is the subordination of self for the good of the whole. Yet, this great good in people is too rarely met with institutional loftiness of purpose, a determination to make a lasting impact, and a wedding of ethical and moral purpose in pursuit of a great good. It is too often subjected to fundraising practices that are petty, shortsighted, manipulative, and, yes, exploitive if not deceitful.

To ensure a brighter future for fundraising, we must take the institutional part of the bargain much more seriously. Institutions must not only stand up for and respond to the best in philanthropy. They must decry and eschew the worst in fundraising. They should resolve that:

- Something so potentially deep should not be treated shallowly.
- Something so potentially good in human nature should not be mined so selfishly.
- Something with the potential of long-term impact should be stunted in the name of short-term need.
- Something so potentially strategic should not be carved up into such small tactical tidbits.
- Something with the potential to unify us in the pursuit and realization of shared aspirations should not be used to divide us or to further narrow our greater affinity.
- Something so lofty should not be brought low.
- Something so priceless should not be cheapened.

The deepest levels of emotional intelligence must take a more prominent place in guiding our fundraising efforts going forward.

Conclusion

The institutions with the greatest potential for future fundraising success will be those that abandon simplistic, short-term assumptions about fundraising and adopt more organic, long-term attitudes and practices designed to build stronger, more sustainable cultures of shared purposes. Below are the practices more institutions must stop and start.

STOP	START
Counting only dollars raised	Counting donors retained
Attributing last year's results to last year's fundraising	Sustaining success through retained relationships
Getting donors to give "annually"	Showing donors how your mission can be advanced every year
Getting donors to conform to your timeline	Accommodating the rhythm and pacing of donors' decision-making
Thinking of donors who didn't give last year as "lapsed"	Thinking of donors who didn't give as mismanaged constituents
Trying to get "lapsed" donors to give again by re-soliciting them	Asking donors who didn't give how you can retain them as constituents
Staging occasional entertainments to raise money	Conducting ongoing conversations to crystalize collective hopes
Fundraising for institutional support	Documenting institutional agency
Asking for more	Projecting greater societal ROI

If fundraising is to become more respected by the most discerning donors and more attractive to the most capable practitioners, the industry must stop pretending to be something it is not and start accepting what it must be.

The more each of us speaks the truth, the more we lighten the burden of false expectations on all of us. The more each of us adopts authentic and considerate practices, the more we will sustain and stem the further drain on the philanthropic spirit that lifts all causes. The more we shed the cloak of mythical persuader and accept the mantle of selfless facilitator, the more joy we will find in our work and the more effective at it we will become.

STOP PRETENDING	START ACCEPTING
Fundraising persuades people to become philanthropic	Without philanthropy fundraising would not be possible
People give because they're asked	People give if they buy into a cause
We're in the gift-getting business	We lose most donors after one gift
Fundraising is best learned from master fundraisers	Fundraising is best learned from listening to discerning donors
Fundraisers are the essential link in donor relations	Fundraisers should help donors develop multiple connections
Successful fundraising ensures an institution's future	Impact ensures an institution's future fundraising success
People have become less generous in responding to institutional need	People have been less credulous about accepting institutional claims
New technology will make fundraisers masters of the philanthropic universe	Most fundraisers struggle to secure appointments with most prospects in their portfolios

When fundraising is done well, it affords the fundraiser, in whatever capacity that might be, the greatest of all privileges –

to see the best of human nature. When conscientious practitioners are afforded that privilege, they know that they have been entrusted with precious cargo. They are transformed from fundraisers into agents of philanthropy, true philanthropy.

True philanthropy is not about money, nor amounts given. It is the clear-eyed conviction that sacrificing a measure of one's individuality is a worthy investment in a world more worthy of vesting one's self in. So much of the hopes of humanity then, you see, hinge on preserving a healthy measure of true philanthropy.

The right way is always the best way in the long run.

APPENDIX: BUT WHAT ABOUT ALL THOSE OTHER "SECRETS OF SUCCESS"?

Ask a thousand people to tell you the keys to fundraising success in the future and you will likely get a thousand answers. Many of them will be right in some sense, but most of them will represent only a part of a larger dynamic and a larger truth. Some of the tools, strategies, and tactics they may emphasize include:

Technology and Data

The term "data analytics" describes the totality of qualitative and quantitative techniques designed to yield insights from huge volumes of data. The term embraces four major areas:

1. *Descriptive Analytics:* A form of statistical analysis that seeks to transform raw data into useful information; usually the first step to yield information from the more advanced form of analytics described below.

2. *Predictive Analytics:* This advanced form of analytics, a tool that has been highly touted in recent years, employs data mining, machine learning, and modeling to predict which donors in an institution's database are most likely to give in the future according to

indicators such as previous giving, years of loyal giving, recent interactions, and other factors.

3. *Diagnostic Analytics:* A retrospective form of analytics, it employs data mining techniques to yield more insight as to how donor behaviors are shifting.

4. *Prescriptive Analytics:* Prescriptive analytics are used to provide advice on data and can inform decision making in the future.

Growing sophistication in this area has allowed fundraising operations to better identify and rank those with the strongest philanthropic potential and insight into their giving propensities. It has also given us aggregate records that will allow fundraisers to build more complete donor records and to manage donor relations over time – which becomes more important as the tenure of fundraisers continue to shorten. Some vendors, however, overstate the capability of their technology and/or have it produce "bells and whistles" reports that seem to satisfy the inner geek in some but provide information that is of tertiary importance, at best.

Advances in digital communications that allow us to reach and interact with constituents on virtual platforms will be of increasing value if used to listen, to converse, not just promote, to put kindred spirits together across time and space, and to create communities of shared purposes and pursuits. Artificial intelligence, the latest craze, which has a strong potential for helping us understand attitudes and behaviors that, if attended to in adroit ways, could help institutions attract donors, lift their philanthropic sights, or even predict when they are most likely to give. However, it will not allow fundraisers to take over donors' brains and direct them to empty their bank accounts into the institutions' unrestricted endowment. Artificial intelligence will aid our ability to adapt to the current and emerging philanthropic realities outlined in this book; it will not make them go away. It will allow us to work more intelligently and identify where the hardest work still needs to be done.

The Importance of Building Relationships with Donors

Yes, but it's not about building relationships for their own sake. It's about being a worthy partner so that good people will want to affiliate with us. More institutions need to be mindful of their fundraising personality and ask themselves why some would want a relationship with someone so desperate, needy, and concerned about the next day that they keep coming back asking for more but never have anything to show for what you've already given them. Or if they would like a relationship with people so full of their own self-importance that they never stop talking about themselves and never show a genuine, unconditional interest in you?

If they give more objective thought to the kind of person that more donors would want to develop a relationship with, they would understand that most humans prefer to develop a relationship with someone who handles adversity with grace and little complaint, who has a promising future and is seeking a long-term partnership, who shares our core values, who proposes ways to work together to achieve a common end, and who is honest and wants honesty in return.

So fundraising isn't just about relationships. It's about fundraising organizations working on developing stronger character and a better future for themselves. As in human relations, we don't go looking for others to make us whole. We make ourselves as whole as we possibly can. We build and pursue our plans for the future. Eventually, the right partners come along, and healthy, productive, and lasting relationships are formed.

Storytelling

Yes, quest narratives are common to every culture at every time, which is proof that a story with a certain structure is of endless appeal. The quest narrative gives a hero, usually representative of some great cause or virtue, "willing to march into hell for a heavenly cause" who must slay the occasional dragon, troll or ogre that gets in his way, yet prevails, either in living form or by sacrificing his life so that the cause might be won. Stories about remarkable people rendering remarkable services to others, particularly if they are emblematic of cultural strength or ethic, therefore, will appeal to and move audiences. However, we must be careful about touting any strategy that is one-sided and assigns talismanic powers to the teller that will mesmerize the listener. Any practice or approach that seeks to wow potential donors into philanthropic submission is counter-relational, if not shallow and selfish. So, it's not just the stories you tell to convey institutional virtues; it's the ones that institutions encourage their prospects and donors to tell. Those with storytelling abilities are of great value to advancement operations but of far greater value are those who engage prospects as if they were their biographers, who:

- Listen for the arc in donors' life stories and the moral they draw from it.
- Begin exploring how their institution could be a part of the next chapter.
- Suggest ways to help them advance their quest.
- Listen for the moment when they begin using the word "we."
- Outline a proposed partnership.
- Listen, negotiate, seek to forge a lasting alliance.
- Prove how iterative, progressive eliciting sessions make soliciting so much more graceful, if necessary at all.

Donor Centrism

The donor-centric school of thought, when applied, can be a highly beneficial correction to fundraising practices that have become too institution-centric (all about "our needs"), or simply too much about fundraising for fundraising's sake. But we must be careful to not over-correct or misinterpret the proper role of donor centrism. Being grateful, respectful, and accountable to donors — and doing all we can to achieve an alignment of interests with them is a critical part of the philanthropic equation. However, entertaining and accepting gifts, or gift conditions, that do not strengthen institutional core competencies, or potentially weaken them, is putting the donor-delight cart in front of the mission-realization horse. We can't correct one imbalance by creating another one. Creating a lasting and productive philanthropic union requires mutual consideration and the willingness of each partner to subordinate individual interests for the sake of achieving shared goals.

Splashy Presentations

Increasingly, donors are asking for more "how" and less "wow" in white papers, proposals, and cases for support. In particular, they are asking how your organization proposes to:

- Tighten its focus to ensure greater mission realization.
- Convert private support into significant, sustainable societal outcomes.
- Relate the dollar amounts requested to specific outcomes.
- Evaluate and report on the progress being made on projects they have funded.
- Adjust and adapt to current and emerging societal trends.

Successful fundraising, in light of these expectations, must be:

- Less mass-marketed, more micro-targeted.
- Lower in gloss, higher in content.
- Less dependent on adverbs, more reliant on action items.
- Less about telling, more about resonance.

Adhering to these new realities will make for more responsive and relevant organizations, not just improved fundraising results. Indeed, being more responsive and striving for greater relevance will be essential to sustaining and securing organizations' "market share" of private support in a declining philanthropic market.

Splashy Events: The Flaws with Fundraising Events

The most successful fundraising comes from iterative, interpersonal discussion; no one-time event will ever achieve as much as deliberate dialogue in optimizing the giving potential of any prospect.

Many events develop their own following – golf tournaments that draw those more interested in playing 18 than in helping an at-risk teen or galas that attract those more interested in showcasing gowns than in coping with Downs.

Sponsors fill the tables or foursomes they buy with their constituents, not yours.

Therefore:

- Don't use events to raise money from causal observers; use them to curate the conscientious and cultivate those with shared convictions.

- Don't provide expensive entertainment, offer substantive, soul-moving experiences that money can't buy.

- Don't rent fancy offsite facilities, bring your donors onsite and inside. Grittiness can be more moving than prettiness.

- Don't tell them about your mission, show them how you are fulfilling it.

- Don't just present, discuss.

Conclusion

There are, of course, even more theories about the keys to achieving fundraising success that are largely or completely wrong. They are the ones that characterize fundraising as a hunting, not a growing, exercise.

> **HUNTERS AND GROWERS**
>
> *Hunters* believe, "The more we get out 'into the field' or commit ourselves to being 'road warriors,' and the more we ask, the better our chances of meeting or exceeding our annual goals."
>
> *Growers* believe, "The more we nurture the good in people by listening respectfully to them, aligning our interests with them, and delivering on our promises to them, the more bountiful our shared harvests will be over time."
>
> The first school likes to "be armed" with stunning presentations in hopes of over-awing their "targets" and "suspects" and praises fundraisers for their ability to "pull the trigger" (i.e., to ask).
>
> The second school stresses the need to "keep our ears close to the ground (i.e., to listen), to "plant seeds" of potential partnerships, and to "to cultivate" the root system of each donor's philanthropic orientation.

There are, of course, blends of the two, but one can see a strong tilt to one or the other in most operations. While each side can mount evidence to support its approach, it seems clear, on the face of it, which is more practical, cost-effective, and sustainable. Hunting thins out the population each year; growing replenishes and increases yield over time. The loss of 20 million households in the past two decades suggests we need much fewer hunters and many more growers.

So, what's the whole truth? What's the real secret to fundraising?

It's this: without philanthropy, there could be no philanthropy. Ergo, the secret to fundraising success is providing what philanthropy feeds, if not feasts, on – to use the good in their lives to make a difference for others.

Additional Reads

Deborah Ancona and Hal Gregersen. "The Power of Leaders Who Focus on Solving Problems." *Harvard Business Review.* April 16, 2018.

Helen Brown. "Prospect research can be stewardship's best friend." January 10, 2019. The Helen Brown Group.

Francesca Gino. "Cracking the Code of Sustained Collaboration." *Harvard Business Review.* November–December 2019 Issue.

Jim Lord. "So I asked Dave Dunlop, Is 'moves management' misunderstood?'" *Leadership Philanthropy.*

"Daniel Pink: The best salespeople aren't extroverts." *The Dallas Morning News.* February 1, 2013.

Nicole Wallace. "'Modern Donors' Are Changing How Charities Should Raise Money." *The Chronicle of Philanthropy.* April 10, 2018.

Jerry Yang → VJ or Tina?
Li Lu
Steve Ballmer Host in SEA
Elaine Wynn - Phnom
Bezos — Carney
Christin

~~Lynne~~ LA
MBKA Engagement → Apr/May/June

ABOUT THE AUTHOR

James M. Langley

Before forming his own comprehensive advancement consulting firm, Jim served as vice president for advancement at Georgetown University. At Georgetown, he led the institution's offices of alumni affairs, strategic communications and marketing, development, medical center development, and advancement services. During his tenure, he produced record numbers in new commitments and dollars. He also launched a number of innovative programs, including the acclaimed Student Discovery Initiative.

Jim arrived at Georgetown after spending eight years as the vice president for advancement at the University of California, San Diego. At UCSD, he led the planning and execution of the institution's seven-year $1 billion campaign, then raised almost half the target amount in three years. Jim also previously served as vice president for external affairs at Georgia Institute of Technology, increasing annual gift income from $26 million to $76 million and more than tripling the institution's endowment to well over $500 million. Operations under his management have won awards in virtually every area of university advancement.

~~Steve~~
~~Jessica Chot~~
Obama Fondess
E Yuan US Leaders
~~TY Bleich~~
DS · TY Bleich
Kopcho
~~Rubbermaid TY Larson~~

March 9 names → to Lidsay ?
                            Erik

DS skiing Tee up

→ Brad & Kathy Smith
  · Amazon

8 slides →

                    ✓ 818 481-2414
DS Email →
Then   ~~818 481~~
                    707 228 2602

E Yuan, Get in front of Strauss re Kori on P44
                                    legacy of
[Warriors game?   climate.
  New names (add)   VBS

                    March 9 → VJ → Doug McG
                    1:1 ⇒
Tmrw → send list to   Eric Yuan →
  DS w/ our names.   ~~Ben~~ DoorDash guys
ADD Godeau. ADD Sean Parker / Evan Spiegel   Ken Lin →